Shakespeare in Three Dimensions

In *Shakespeare in Three Dimensions*, Robert Blacker asks us to set aside what we think we know about Shakespeare and rediscover his plays on the page, and as Shakespeare intended, in the rehearsal room and in performance. That process includes stripping away false traditions that have obscured his observations about people and social institutions that are still vital to our lives today. This book explores the verities of power and love in *Romeo and Juliet* and *Macbeth*, as an example of how to mine the extraordinary detail in all of Shakespeare's plays, using the knowledge of both theatre practitioners and scholars to excavate and restore them.

Robert Blacker was the first dramaturg at Joseph Papp's Public Theater in New York City, and Des McAnuff's associate artistic director and dramaturg at the Tony-award-winning La Jolla Playhouse for twelve seasons, where he worked on *The Who's Tommy* and Steppenwolf's *Grapes of Wrath*. Over fifty projects from Blacker's eight years as artistic director of the Sundance Theatre Labs went on to production, including *I Am My Own Wife* and *The Laramie Project*. He worked on 20 productions of Shakespeare at these theatres and the Stratford Shakespeare Festival of Canada, where he was insitutional dramaturg for five seasons. He has taught Shakespeare studies in graduate theatre programs at Columbia, Iowa, UCSD, and the Yale School of Drama, where he was interim chair of playwriting. His interview is the first of eighty-five articles in *The Routledge Companion to Dramaturgy* (2015). He is a graduate of Cornell University.

Focus on Dramaturgy
Series Editor: Magda Romanska

www.routledge.com/performance/series/RFOD

The role of the dramaturg is increasingly central to contemporary theatre-making. The *Focus on Dramaturgy* series provides a forum for scholars and professionals from across the world of dramaturgical practice to reflect on the discipline's key questions. From dramaturgical approaches to Shakespeare or the dramaturgy of sound, to theatre-making in migrant communities and televisual media, this collection of essays, manifestos and discussions brings together a rich blend of voices on one of theatre's central disciplines.

Shakespeare in Three Dimensions

The Dramaturgy of *Macbeth* and *Romeo and Juliet*

Robert Blacker

LONDON AND NEW YORK

First published 2018
by Routledge
2 Park Square, Milton Park, Abingdon, Oxon OX14 4RN

and by Routledge
605 Third Avenue, New York, NY 10017

First issued in paperback 2020

Routledge is an imprint of the Taylor & Francis Group, an informa business

British Library Cataloguing-in-Publication Data
A catalogue record for this book is available from the British Library

Library of Congress Cataloging-in-Publication Data
Names: Blacker, Robert, author.
Title: Shakespeare's dramaturgy : a case study of Romeo and Juliet and Macbeth / Robert Blacker.
Description: Abingdon, Oxon ; New York, NY : Routledge, 2018. | Includes bibliographical references and index.
Identifiers: LCCN 2017031198 | ISBN 9781138284531 (hardback : alk. paper) | ISBN 9781351979009 (web pdf) | ISBN 9781351978996 (epub) | ISBN 9781351978989 (kindle)
Subjects: LCSH: Shakespeare, William, 1564–1616—Criticism, Textual. | Shakespeare, William, 1564–1616. Romeo and Juliet. | Shakespeare, William, 1564–1616. Macbeth.
Classification: LCC PR3071 .B47 2018 | DDC 822.3/3—dc23
LC record available at https://lccn.loc.gov/2017031198

ISBN 13: 978-0-367-73571-5 (pbk)
ISBN 13: 978-1-138-28453-1 (hbk)

Typeset in Times New Roman
by Apex CoVantage, LLC

This book is dedicated to Des McAnuff, who led the way

Contents

Foreword

Robert Blacker was the first person to use the title of dramaturg at Joseph Papp's Public Theatre and its Shakespeare in the Park in New York, where we first met and worked together. Mr. Papp took the title of producer, but he functioned as *de facto* dramaturg on many of his productions, working closely with playwrights and directors. It is testimony to Robert's artistic talents and erudition that he was recognized in this way.

We have worked together as director/dramaturg in partnership on a dozen productions of Shakespeare and supervised many others as leaders of institutional theaters, such as the La Jolla Playhouse and Stratford Festival of Canada. Early in our journey together, we coined the term "sleuthing" as a way to describe the work on a play that would begin many months in advance of rehearsal and sometimes continued through the run of the play. Over the next decades, Robert has continued to hone his skills on twenty productions of Shakespeare. His extensive work as dramaturg with living writers has deeply influenced his understanding of playwriting and so his approach to the classics. Robert is one of the few individuals who have spent equal amounts of time in the rehearsal room and the research library, and his book reminds us that dramaturgy is a continuing process that includes both. *Shakespeare in Three Dimensions* will be of interest to anyone who loves the plays of William Shakespeare but it is of particular value to practitioners – actors, directors, dramaturgs and designers, and other theatre artists.

Reading this book is rather like diving into a detective story four hundred years after the event. Every time someone embarks on a new performance of Shakespeare's plays it is necessary to take nothing for granted. For example, in one of our first productions, John Vickery, the actor who was playing Romeo, asked the unthinkable – does Romeo love Juliet? While at first, on the surface, the answer may seem obvious, upon reflection it would be fair to say "no" and "yes." Romeo enters the play in love with Rosaline and almost instantly falls head over heels for Juliet, leading one to the possible conclusion that he is more in love with love itself than the actual girl. By the fifth act of the play, he has matured and transformed; his feelings have changed profoundly and there is little question that he loves the woman that he ends up giving his life for.

Shakespeare in Three Dimensions should inspire contemporary theatre artists to question the assumptions they take into production on any of his plays and transcend prejudices that have developed over centuries. It is not enough to depend on the insights of scholars and regurgitate past discoveries. All essential information about story and character is contained in the text in order to illuminate our *own* times.

The great director Michael Langham was adamant that Shakespeare's plays were meant to be performed and not simply read. In order to be truly understood, the words need to be spoken aloud. Shakespeare created *Romeo and Juliet* at a time when he was presumably trying to prove himself to his university-educated peers. It is Shakespeare, as Langham described, drunk on words, showing off his virtuosic ability as a poet in order to prove himself. *Macbeth*, which premiered a decade later, reveals a dramatist who is less interested in showing off his astonishing language skills and more focused on achieving a profound depth in character, theme, and storytelling. While this book focuses mainly on these two texts, they work in tandem to give us the perfect litmus test for the complete works of William Shakespeare.

Robert's description of text analysis is an instrument meant to be used for dissection, not a pat interpretation of either play. The six productions of these two plays he has worked on have been considerably varied, and there is little danger that any keen artist would simply follow in his footsteps and come to identical conclusions. The investigative journey is what is important here. A serious student of Shakespeare should be able to take the lead from Robert's approach and set out on an adventure of discovery that comes from combining careful research with the rigor of the rehearsal process, and culminating in the ultimate work done there in the space between the actors.

One of Shakespeare's greatest breakthroughs as a dramatist is that he managed to create a matrix of points of view without seeming to judge the individuals that he was portraying. In other words, he was able to create a theatrical blueprint for life itself. The great revelations of Shakespeare's plays can ultimately only come from doing them, but this book should help anyone who wants to explore these plays to become a formidable sleuth, whether as practitioner or admirer.

Des McAnuff

Acknowledgments

I am deeply indebted to Peter Brook and Joseph Papp for introducing me to the splendors of Shakespeare. I have learned about these plays by watching Brook's productions, both live and on film, and from working with directors and actors on twenty productions at Papp's Public Theatre and Shakespeare in the Park (New York), at the La Jolla Playhouse (California), and the Stratford Festival of Canada.

I want to thank these colleagues for their advice and support during the writing of this book: Elinor Fuchs, Jacob Gallagher-Ross, James Leverett, Des McAnuff, and Doug Wright. Sharon Dynak and her staff at the Ucross Foundation provided me with an environment where I could focus on my writing in the austere beauty of the Wyoming plateau. I especially want to thank Magda Romanska for her suggestions and for her advocacy both of this series and my book, as well as Ben Piggott and his staff at Routledge for their kindness and patience.

*****

Introduction

There is an engraving of Shakespeare on the title page of the First Folio of his plays. Opposite it is a sonnet by fellow playwright Ben Jonson. He suggests that if we want to discover Shakespeare we should "looke / Not on his Picture, but his Booke."[1] That is the best advice on mounting his plays that I have found and the argument of the book that follows. The engraving of Shakespeare was made after his death. Four hundred years of writing about these plays have created many other portraits of him as well. Some have been essential to productions that I have worked on: none are the plays themselves. My book asks you to set aside your picture of Shakespeare and what you think you know about his work. Begin by reading his plays uncut and continue to explore them in three dimensions, as Shakespeare intended, in the rehearsal room and in performance. You may find something different than what you thought, or have been told, is there.

Mounting Shakespeare for the stage today is a process of stripping away the 400 years that separate us from the time of the writing of his plays in order to reveal the brilliance of his observations about people and social institutions. That length of time can be daunting. The meaning of words has changed: Jonson's sonnet praises Shakespeare for his "wit," which in their time also meant "mind" and "understanding."[2] Customs in writing and in society have changed. People, however, have not. Shakespeare was such an astute and unsentimental observer that his characters and situations are still familiar to us. Some people prefer the Sistine Chapel frescoes before they were cleaned to the brilliant colors that the cleaning revealed; some prefer breeches on the genitalia of "The Last Judgment" there. Removing the accumulation of centuries always has detractors who prefer nostalgia and taste to the search for truth.

To understand Shakespeare's plays, it is necessary to become familiar with the tools of his formidable dramaturgy. In the first half of this book, I focus on the more traditional elements of text analysis and examine the words on the pages of *Romeo and Juliet*, as an example. I hope practitioners and admirers of Shakespeare will find something new in this underestimated play. I also survey basic elements of his craft for students of Shakespeare of all ages and for those who are new to mounting his plays.

In Part Two, I examine *Macbeth* and the elements of Shakespeare's dramaturgy that confront us when his plays are put on their feet. Analysis that is limited to the page is never sufficient: the rehearsal room is also a research facility. Those of us who work there often do not record our discoveries, and so they are lost when a production closes. This book attempts to address that and to encourage other practitioners to share what they have learned in this period. Context is also important in approaching a playwright who is interested in how the public and private spheres intersect in his plays. Shakespeare is recording the issues of his times through the lens of his personal preoccupations. Knowledge of the environment in which his plays were written is essential to fully understanding their relevance both then and today. Knowledge of their production history is also important, and even critical with *Macbeth*, as false traditions still affect our perception of that play. Both of these areas will take us into the vast writing on Shakespeare. My notes will point you to some of the outstanding scholars who influenced the productions I have worked on.

I chose to examine *Romeo and Juliet* and *Macbeth* because both observe Shakespeare's two great preoccupations: power and love. Yes, *Macbeth* is also a love story, and *Romeo and Juliet* presents two powerful families locked in violence. They also provide examples from different periods in Shakespeare's career. Writers evolve, and what may pertain to a playwright earlier in his/her career may not be entirely applicable later.

This book is a record of where these two plays live for me after six encounters with them in production. Equally important, my text analysis serves as an example of the extraordinary detail that you will find in Shakespeare's plays. It is your attention to that detail which will lead you to discover where his plays live for you, without creating reductive versions of them.

In his celebrated book, Jan Kott demonstrates that Shakespeare is our contemporary.[3] Shakespeare's plays are still relevant to our contemporary concerns and issues, if we take the time to confront them fully – in reading them, in conversations with our collaborators, on our feet in rehearsal, and finally with the contributions of an audience. Whatever your approach to production, whether traditional or postmodern, "making Shakespeare relevant" begins by recognizing all that is relevant in his plays. Those acts of recognition are the subject of this book.

Notes

1 *The Norton Facsimile: The First Folio of Shakespeare*, ed. Charlton Hinman (Norton, 1968), p. 2. The First Folio is the first *collected* edition of Shakespeare's plays, published in 1623.

2 *Oxford English Dictionary* (Oxford University Press, 1971), wit, sb. I.1 and 2.
3 Jan Kott, *Shakespeare Our Contemporary* (Norton, 1964).

Bibliography

For the productions of *Romeo and Juliet* and *Macbeth* at La Jolla Playhouse in 1983 and 1989 respectively, we used the Arden editions, edited by Brian Gibbons (1980) and Kenneth Muir (1951). For productions of those plays at the Stratford Shakespeare Festival of Canada in 2008 and 2009, we used more recent editions in the Oxford World's Classics series, edited by Jill L. Levenson (2000) and Nicholas Brooke (1990), which I quote in this book. In addition, the Bedford/St. Martin editions contain extensive research on the environment in which the plays were written. Footnotes on Shakespeare's text identify passages by act, scene and line number.

Sources cited

Kott, Jan. *Shakespeare Our Contemporary*. Norton, 1964.

The Norton Facsimile: The First Folio of Shakespeare. Ed. Charlton Hinman. Norton, 1968.

Oxford English Dictionary. Oxford University Press, 1971.

Part I

Romeo and Juliet

What's in a word?

1 The boys

Two men enter. Some older editions call the men servants, but most contemporary editors use the words of the authoritative published version, the Second Quarto of 1599.[1] It designates the men simply as "of the house of Capulet." We never learn what their position within the household is, but rank is important to them. Something has happened offstage. They have been insulted, and they do not want to be seen as menials. As parentheses occur in Shakespeare's texts, I use brackets to add definitions and complete phrases to explicate the text: these are not suggestions for changes. I also italicize words to make points, such as the series of homophonic puns below, which begin with allusions to class:[2]

SAMSON Gregory, on my word we'll not carry *coals* ["do dirty work;" proverbially, "put up with insults"].[3]
GREGORY No, for then we should be *colliers* ["who carry coals for sale"].[4]
SAMSON I mean, an [if] we be in *choler*, we'll draw [our swords].
GREGORY Ay, while you live, draw your neck out of *collar* [a hangman's noose].[5]

Samson and Gregory are often performed as if they are the same character, but Shakespeare differentiates characters, even in smaller roles. The Murderers in *Macbeth* are differentiated, for example, and their scene with Macbeth is built around this difference. Shakespeare was an actor and understood how to write for actors. The difference between his characters creates a tension that gives scenes their shape. Here, the appropriately named Samson continually flaunts his machismo, and Gregory, who enjoys taunting him and provoking him, repeatedly deflates his macho posturing:

SAMSON I strike quickly being moved [to do so].
GREGORY But thou are not quickly moved to strike.
SAMSON A dog of the house of Montague moves me.

GREGORY To move is to stir, and to be valiant is to stand [and fight]: therefore if thou art moved thou runn'st away.
SAMSON A dog of that house shall move me to stand.[6]

The wordplay here is intense. In Shakespeare, people of all classes play with words: this should come as no surprise to us in the age of rap. In this dialogue, Samson and Gregory repeat each other's words – moved, quickly, stand – and expand or twist their meanings.[7] The actors must listen closely to each other in order to do this. Carol Burnett told me that another great comedian, Lucille Ball, said the key to her timing was to listen to the other actor. This is essential to performing Shakespeare, whether the scene is comedic or dramatic. Shakespeare's lines build off each other. His scenes build off each other. His drama proceeds from what has happened before. Shakespeare is a master of this, and it is fundamental both to dramatic writing and to understanding Shakespeare's art. The key to an elusive line can usually be found in the ones that precede it.

Samson next asserts his prowess with women. Shakespeare typically is direct about sex. Samson says he will push Montague's men into the gutter, which in Elizabethan England would be filled with garbage and manure, and "thrust his maids to the wall," where they will enjoy his "piece of flesh."[8] Shakespeare understood that threats of violence are often cloaked in sexual innuendo. For his part, Gregory replies that Samson's piece of flesh is poor fare.

Note how Shakespeare now exposes Samson and Gregory. Two Montagues now enter, and what do Samson and Gregory do? These macho men decide to *frown* at the Montagues as they pass. They are only willing to insult the Montagues openly when they see another Capulet – Tybalt – offstage, and numbers are on their side. Shakespeare ends their part of the scene by revealing the emptiness of Samson and Gregory's bravado. This gives the scene a progression. The "tragedy" of *Romeo and Juliet* as it is called both in folio and quarto editions begins with a satiric scene that is an astute critique of machismo.

Swords are now drawn, but another Montague, Benvolio, enters before Tybalt. Benvolio draws his sword to part the two factions, but this is a mistake. In the violent world of this play, the peacemakers are ineffective because they are inevitably drawn into the fight. Romeo repeats this pattern in the middle of the play. Repetition of patterns is key to dramatic structure. Here, in the opening scene, Tybalt enters and sees that Benvolio has drawn his sword. This gives him an excuse to challenge Benvolio. Tybalt is appalled that Benvolio would fight men beneath his social class, but he will fight Benvolio:

> What, art thou drawn among these heartless hinds?
> Turn thee, Benvolio, look upon thy death.[9]

"Heartless hinds" is a semantic pun: each word has two meanings. The phrase means menials (hinds) without courage (heart), as well as female deer (hinds) without a male (hart) to protect them. Tybalt insults these men by calling them both cowardly menials and, in his eyes, defenseless women, and so the brawl begins. Throughout the play violence is associated with derogatory expressions of social and sexual status – still the language of machismo today.

Ralph Berry writes in *Shakespeare and Social Class*:

> The entire action is presented through the class register. Tybalt, for example, enters the play on a class note, "What, are thou drawn among these heartless hinds?" . . . and leaves it on a sneer of the same order, "Thou wretched boy, that dids't consort with him here, / Shalt with him hence." . . . In between he has received some rough handling from his host at the party: Capulet's address turns rapidly from "gentle coz" to "goodman boy"; (which places him below a yeoman) . . . In choler, these people reach first for the epithet of class disdain.[10]

A yeoman "cultivates his own land" but a goodman is "a tenant of a specified estate or farm, *obsolete*," Berry notes.[11] The choice of words is important in Shakespeare.

The Citizens of Verona now enter and cry out: "Down with the Capulets, down with the Montagues!"[12] It is easy to understand why they are so upset. The enmity between the two households has "thrice disturbed the quiet of our streets,"[13] as the Prince will tell us when he enters. The wreckage from the brawl must be considerable enough to earn Romeo's comment on it when he enters.

But first, Capulet enters in his dressing gown, which indicates that it is early morning. His two-line exchange with his wife is packed with detail about them. The Lord and Lady designations for the Capulets and Montagues that appear in older editions of this play are not in the First Folio or the authoritative Second Quarto (see Chapter 2). They are wealthy, but not necessarily nobility. The Oxford World's Classics edition uses these designations and this formatting to distinguish verse passages:

CAPULET
What noise is this? Give me my long sword, ho!
CAPULET'S WIFE
A crutch, a crutch – why call you for a sword?[14]

The out-of-date long sword was useless in the time of the lightweight rapier. It suggests Capulet's age. His wife's reprimand indicates the state of their marriage. She does not hesitate to mock him in public. Montague's Wife holds back her husband with more neutral words: "Thou shalt not stir one foot to seek a foe."[15] Shakespeare begins to define the nature of these two relationships right from the beginning.

The Prince now enters with his entourage. The length of his speech has a dramatic purpose: his presence is not enough to end the fighting. The Prince's anger – "Will they not hear?"[16] – expresses his frustration that it takes him eight lines of verse to bring the brawl to an end. Shakespeare often puts important stage directions into his dialogue. The Prince too is punished for his inability to keep the peace. There are really three households in *Romeo and Juliet*, and each loses "a brace [two] of kinsmen."[17] Mercutio and Paris are the Prince's cousins, and these relationships become critical to understanding Shakespeare's play. The Prince now tells Montague and Capulet that their "lives shall pay the forfeit of the peace," if this happens again.[18] He asks Capulet to go with him and asks Montague to meet with him later. Details are significant in Shakespeare. As we learn later Capulet is the more volatile of the two: perhaps the Prince knows he must deal with him immediately.

Shakespeare's plays cannot fully speak to us if we make cuts before we understand the purpose of that material. Sampson and Gregory and the brawl that follows are the playwright's invention. What Shakespeare brings to the table and how his plays differ from their source materials give us insight into the play.[19] Jill L. Levenson writes: "Shakespeare dramatized a story familiar to his audience through popular sources for at least thirty years."[20] The opening scene is usually cut so drastically because directors fail to recognize that it sets up a world of men who behave like boys, a point of view that we can still understand today. Samson and Gregory, Tybalt and Benvolio, Capulet and Montague all contribute to understanding this pattern. Shakespeare actually outlines it in the opening lines of the play.

Two households, two lovers, two stories

Romeo and Juliet opens with a sonnet: "Two households both alike in dignity . . .". Three quatrains of alternating rhyme are followed by a couplet. According to the *Oxford English Dictionary*, dignity can mean both "the quality of being worthy," the sense in which we use it today, and "degree of estimation, rank."[21] The issue of rank raised by Sampson and Gregory is actually introduced in the first line of the play.

A good dictionary such as the *OED* is the most important tool in understanding Shakespeare's plays. Look for one that gives archaic meanings of words and offers multiple choices as to meaning. Shakespearean glossaries are helpful, but they can become a dangerous crutch if they choose one meaning for a word in a given line, rather than allowing you to make that choice. And always remember, Shakespeare is a poet and may be juggling more than one meaning.

The Prologue actually tells us there are *two* stories in the play, in carefully constructed alternating passages of equal length. I have italicized the lines that refer to the second story to underscore the equal time Shakespeare gives to both:

> Two households both alike in dignity,
>   In fair Verona, where we lay our scene,
> From ancient grudge break to new mutiny,
>   Where civil blood makes civil hands unclean.
> *From forth the fatal loins of these two foes*
>   *A pair of star-crossed lovers take their life,*
> *Whose misadventured piteous overthrows*
>   *Doth with their death bury their parents' strife.*
> *The fearful passage of their death-marked love*
>   And the continuance of their parents' rage –
> *Which but their children's end naught could remove –*
>   Is now the two hours' traffic of our stage;
> The which if you with patient ears attend,
> What here shall miss, our toil shall strive to mend.[22]

When Des McAnuff and I first sat down to discuss his upcoming production at the La Jolla Playhouse in 1983, we were surprised by how much of the play we had never seen onstage. Most productions cut the play to focus on the love story because they do not appreciate the sophistication of *Romeo and Juliet*'s public story and its continued relevance today. We know "the continuance of their parents' rage" is a public story because "mutiny" implies damage to the ship of state. "Civil," meaning citizens, confirms this and "civil blood" tells us what that damage can be.

We never discover the source of the feud because the play is not about a feud. In fact, that word does not occur in the play. Shakespeare uses "grudge," which implies something petty or slight. The *OED* defines that word as "grumbling" and "dissatisfaction." It also adds an obsolete meaning: "resentment due to . . . the superiority of an opponent or rival," which sits comfortably with the class disdain that permeates the opening sequences and becomes important to the public story of the play.[23] "Continuance," by the way, is an active word. It implies something continuing into the present. The sonnet promises that we will see what fuels "their parents' rage," in the present. What's in a word? With Shakespeare, as we will continue to see, there is quite a lot.

It is important to note that neither of the title characters is present in the sequence of events described so far in the play. When Romeo enters, he remarks on the detritus left on stage from the brawl. He equates the chaos the brawl has caused with the turmoil of his unrequited love for an as yet unnamed person in a passage that moves back and forth between the two:

> . . . What fray was here?
> Yet tell me not, for I have heard it all [before]:
> Here's much to do with hate [the brawl], but more with love.
> Why then, O brawling love, O loving hate,
> O anything of nothing first created:
> O heavy lightness, serious vanity,
> Mis-shapen chaos of well-seeming forms,
> Feather of lead, bright smoke, cold fire, sick-health,
> Still-waking sleep that is not what it is:
> This love feel I that feel no love in this [the brawl].[24]

Which lines refer to the fray and which refer to Romeo's state of mind is confusing, because his state of mind is confused. Actors can make differing valid choices. What is clear is that, at the minimum, Romeo begins and ends the speech by referring to the "continuance of their parents' rage." His conclusion, "that feel no love in this," is his point of departure in the *public* story of the play. As with Prince Hal at the beginning of *Henry IV* or Michael Corleone at the beginning of *The Godfather*, Romeo absents himself from the family business, for reasons beyond his preoccupation with Rosaline.

Shakespeare often juxtaposes public and private stories in his plays because he was interested in how the public sphere, political and societal, affects our daily lives, and how individuals can alter the course of events. Critical writing on his plays is often based on viewing productions that have cut out important sections of his texts, often in the public stories because they may be more difficult to identify 400 years later. Over time this fossilizes into false traditions that distort the plays and fail to realize their full scope and beauty. The Prologue promises that we will see a public story about power. The texts we have examined so far are just the first installment.

Points of departure

We are now in the world of the love stories. I am using the plural because Romeo actually has two loves, Juliet has two suitors, and the Capulets, sadly, have each other. Romeo's parents asked Benvolio to find out the reason for his absence. When Romeo enters, he tells Benvolio that he is in love but that his love is not returned. Suddenly, Romeo interrupts his melancholy lament with these words: "Where shall we dine?"[25] This interjection is so odd for the supposedly love-preoccupied Romeo that it should make us question the nature of that love. In their first scene together, Friar Laurence will also question Romeo's love for Rosaline: "O she knew well, / Thy love did read by rote, that could not spell."[26]

Romeo's interruption should also make us laugh. *Romeo and Juliet* is listed among the tragedies in the Folio, but by the time Shakespeare wrote it he was experimenting with form: "It is hard for us to realize the full extent of [*Romeo and Juliet's*] novelty. . . . Romance was the stuff of the comic stage."[27] The first half of the play is arguably a comedy, and scenes such as Samson and Gregory's as well as Romeo's are replete with ironic humor. Mercutio's scenes, as we shall see, raise wit to new heights in the play. That comedic tone abruptly changes with the deaths halfway through the play. Today, we accept this kind of shift because we are familiar with it in contemporary theatre, but it has taken the last hundred years to throw off sentimental Victorian notions about *Romeo and Juliet*, which stressed its romantic side and reduced its complexity.

As his scene with Benvolio goes on, we find a Romeo who is not the romantic lover of Victorian stage tradition, but a teenage boy who bemoans Rosaline's commitment to chastity: "She will not . . . ope her lap to saint-seducing gold" has two meanings.[28] After he meets Juliet at the ball, Romeo asks: "Can I go forward when my heart is here?"[29] How are we to take his sudden turn of affections to Juliet? Friar Laurence confronts him about this: "Holy Saint Francis, what a change is here! / Young men's love then lies / Not truly in their hearts, but in their eyes."[30]

We discussed that question during rehearsals for our production at the La Jolla Playhouse. That a teenage boy should so suddenly change his affections should not surprise us, but given his passionate feelings about Rosaline how real is this new love for Juliet? What kind of love is it – at the beginning of the play? This is his point of departure in the *private* story of *Romeo and Juliet*: how does it change during the course of the play?

Shakespeare continues to observe the mechanisms of love in the next scene. When we next see Capulet he is in conversation with Paris, who wants permission to court Juliet. Capulet tells Paris that she is too young for marriage, and he seems to be speaking about his experience with his wife: "Too soon marred are those so early made. / Earth has swallowed up all my hopes but she [Juliet]."[31] Both Paris's and Romeo's courtships of Juliet are set against Shakespeare's portrait of the unhappy Capulet marriage. The multiple stories of *Romeo and Juliet*, as we shall continue to see, allow Shakespeare to examine love in many different aspects.

Capulet loves his daughter and calls her "the hopeful lady of my earth."[32] He seems genuinely conflicted about allowing her to marry, but his lengthy portrait of Juliet as an unmatchable catch also suggests that he may be encouraging Paris's interest. That was McAnuff's choice in his production at La Jolla. After all, "County" Paris is a kinsman to the Prince. He has the rank, the connections, and money: Capulet's Wife refers to him in the next scene as a "golden story."[33] Gold becomes an important image in the last third of the play, and its connection to Paris here sets that up. Whatever choice we make, after the death of Mercutio, another kinsman to the Prince, Capulet *orders* Juliet to marry Paris. The marriage becomes a strategic necessity. Capulet too goes on a journey that has its point of departure here.

Shakespeare's texts contain a wealth of detail that is rarely fully mined. In these opening sequences, Shakespeare observes the mechanisms of love and violence, as they exist at the beginning of the play. He shows us how bravado can slip into violence and that both are often tied to class disdain and social and sexual insecurities, patterns that he will continue to explore throughout the play. Shakespeare also reminds us that boys can be as old as Capulet, who at his ball that evening tells his guests, "I have seen the day / That I have worn a visor and could tell / A whispering tale in a fair lady's ear," and soon thereafter breaks into his tantrum at Tybalt.[34]

Harry Levin has pointed out that the kind of sequence that opens the play is repeated twice.[35] I would add that these three sequences are remarkably similar in structure. Someone enters in a foul mood, there is a challenge, and swords are drawn. Someone tries to stop the violence, and the Prince enters to no avail. These scenes occur at the beginning and end of the play, and right in the middle. With an exponentially increasing death toll, they create a dramatic structure that carries forward the public story that we will examine in more detail later. Romeo and Juliet are absent from the first of these scenes. Romeo is present in the second; both are present in the third. They are literally drawn into the violence of the public story in the play. In subsequent chapters we will examine how.

Notes

1 A quarto is a single-play edition. For the relationship between quartos and folios, see Chapter Two.
2 Homophonic puns use words that sound the same. In a semantic pun, one word has two meanings: see p. 8.
3 *Romeo and Juliet*, ed. Jill L. Levenson (Oxford World's Classics, 2000), notes on 1.1.1.
4 Ibid., note on 1.1.2.
5 Ibid., 1.1.1–4. For extended dialogue from Oxford editions, I follow its formatting, which indicates *prose* passage, as here, by setting speech prefixes on the

same line. For *verse* passages, speech prefixes are set on a separate line. See note 14.

6 *Romeo and Juliet*, ed. Levenson, 1.1.5–10.
7 These repetitions are examples of the use of rhetoric, as described in Chapter Five.
8 *Romeo and Juliet*, ed. Levenson, 1.1.16–17 and 28.
9 Ibid., 1.1.62–63.
10 Ralph Berry, *Shakespeare and Social Class* (Humanities Press, 1988), p. 42. Berry's book is indispensible for understanding class relationships that may be lost to us today.
11 *Oxford English Dictionary* (Oxford University Press, 1971), goodman 4b; yeoman, II.4.
12 *Romeo and Juliet*, ed. Levenson, 1.1.70.
13 Ibid., 1.1.87.
14 Ibid., 1.1.71–72. I follow Oxford's formatting of *verse* passages, which sets speech prefixes on a separate line. For the formatting of prose passages, see note 5.
15 Ibid., 1.1.76.
16 Ibid., 1.1.79.
17 Ibid., 5.3.295. A brace indicates two.
18 Ibid., 1.1.93.
19 Bill Bryson writes that only in *Midsummer*, *Love's Labour's Lost* and *The Tempest* does Shakespeare "appear to have borrowed from no one." Bryson, *Shakespeare: The World as Stage* (Atlas Books, 2007), pp. 99–100.
20 *Romeo and Juliet*, ed. Levenson, p. 15. In this excellent edition used for our Stratford production, Levenson meticulously outlines how one version begat the next: pp. 4–15.
21 *Oxford English Dictionary* (Oxford University Press, 1971), dignity, 1 and 2.
22 *Romeo and Juliet*, ed. Levenson, 1.0.1–14.
23 *Oxford English Dictionary*, grudge, sb. 1 and 3.
24 *Romeo and Juliet*, ed. Levenson, 1.1.169–78.
25 Ibid., 1.1.169.
26 Ibid., 2.2.87–88.
27 Harry Levin, "Form and Formality in 'Romeo and Juliet'," in *Shakespeare and the Revolution of the Times* (Galaxy, 1976), p. 108.
28 *Romeo and Juliet*, ed. Levenson, 1.1.208–10.
29 Ibid., 2.1.1
30 Ibid., 2.2.65–68.
31 Ibid., 1.2.13–14. In the next scene, Capulet's Wife tells Juliet she married at her age.
32 Ibid., 1.2.15.
33 Ibid., 1.3.94.
34 Ibid., 1.4.134–36.
35 Levin, "Form and Formality in 'Romeo and Juliet'," p. 110.

Bibliography

Shakespeare editions cited

Romeo and Juliet. Ed. Jill L. Levenson. Oxford World's Classics, 2000.

Other sources

Berry, Ralph. *Shakespeare and Social Class*. Humanities Press, 1988.
Bryson, Bill. *Shakespeare: The World as Stage*. Atlas Books, 2007.
Levin, Harry. "Form and Formality in 'Romeo and Juliet'." In *Shakespeare and the Revolution of the Times*. Galaxy, 1976.
Oxford English Dictionary. Oxford University Press, 1971.

2 Folios and quartos

Editors of contemporary editions make choices in assembling their texts and you may wish to question some of their choices. For this reason, you need to understand the nature of the original editions of Shakespeare's plays.

Actors often lead the way because they must speak the lines and may sense that something is wrong before a director or dramaturg does. I worked on a production of *The Comedy of Errors* where Jesse Tyler Fergusson asked director Daniel Sullivan to restore some fourth-act cuts we made before rehearsals began.[1] Dromio of Ephesus complains regularly about the abuse of his master, and these lines had initially seemed like more of the same. When we reexamined the speech on its feet and *in the context of the preceding scenes*, we realized that this was the closest this beleaguered slave came to a declaration of independence. The restored lines gave him some growth and allowed him to speak more freely against his master in that act. Shakespeare builds off what has gone before and his lines can seldom be fully understood in isolation.

If the text is primary, where does it come from?

Folios

Eighteen of the thirty-six plays the First Folio contains were printed there for the first time after Shakespeare's death in 1616 and are the sole extant source of these plays. Without the First Folio of 1623, we would not have half of Shakespeare's plays. *Macbeth* is one of them. "Folio" is from the Latin word *folium* or leaf. In folio printing, a sheet of paper is folded once, creating two leaves or four pages for binding.

The Second Folio (1632) was reprinted from the first, with corrections. Some editors cite it if there is a perceived problem with First Folio text because some of the original manuscripts may still have existed at the time of the Second Folio's printing. The Third and Fourth folios (1663/1664 and

1685) are reprints of the previous folios and have little authority. The Third, however, does contain *Pericles*, the first time that play, now considered part of the canon, was printed in a folio.

The Folio (as I will call the First Folio from here on) contains many moving dedications, including the poem by Ben Jonson, cited at the beginning of this book. Publishing a collection of plays was a new idea. Jonson was the first to publish his collected *Works* in 1616, but Shakespeare chose to publish his poems instead. He wrote plays for the present, that instant in time in which theatre lives. The Folio cost one pound; few could afford it.[2] Why was it printed?

Theatre companies

John Heminges and William Condell give us an answer in the first of their Folio dedications. They write that the First Folio was printed "without ambition either of selfe-profit, or fame: onely to keep the memory of so worthy a Friend & Fellow alive, as was our SHAKESPEARE."[3] Their names appear in the Folio's list of the principal actors in Shakespeare's company. Theatre companies at this time were companies of actors. Shakespeare made his principal income as an actor-shareholder in the company and later as a shareholder in the ownership of the Globe Theatre. He sold his plays to the company for a fee, but he retained no rights to them and made no further income from them, because there were no copyright laws to protect playwrights or the theatre companies to whom they sold their plays.

The list of twenty-six actors in the Folio is a compilation of all the actors who shared in the profits of that company until the Folio's publication in 1623. From seven or eight sharers, the Lord Chamberlain's Men, founded in 1594, grew to an average size of twelve by 1603, when their patronage changed and they became the King's Men.[4] The patronage of the new king, James I, was a mark of their success. "From 1576 to 1642 there were never less than two, and sometimes more than five, prosperous [London] theatres competing for weekly audiences of 18,000 to 24,000."[5] The King's Men, however, maintained the distinction of being the only company active throughout the period that ended in 1642, when the Puritans came to power and closed the theatres.

That list of actor-shareholders in the Folio begins with the actor in their company who was also their principal playwright, William Shakespeare.[6] It was followed by Richard Burbage, the company's great tragedian. His father built the first permanent outdoor London playhouse in 1576, for the proto-company that preceded the Lord Chamberlain's Men. It was called, simply, the Theatre, and was located just north of the City. John Heminges' name is listed next on the Folio list. He took over the role of actor-leader of the company after Richard Burbage's death in 1619. Henry Condell is also listed. Both Heminges and Condell received small bequests in Shakespeare's will.

This number of sharers changed as actors left or joined the company. Their principal comedian, Will Kemp, left the company soon after they opened the Globe in 1599 and was replaced by Robert Armin. We know that Kemp played the role of Peter in *Romeo and Juliet* because his name appears in a stage entrance in the Second Quarto. He was a more physical clown than his successor, and Shakespeare wrote to their strengths. Once Armin joined the company, Shakespeare's clowns and fools became more verbal, witty, and philosophical. Armin probably played Touchstone in *As You Like It*, a play that was written on the cusp of the transition from Kemp to Armin, and that is a clue as to how that sophisticated character should be played. In Des McAnuff's 1984 production at the La Jolla Playhouse, which was set in the 1930s, he addressed this by having Touchstone first appear in formal dress with a champagne glass in his hand, the Noel Coward of the court. This made his later complaints about the rural life in the Forest of Arden all the more funny. The appearance of actors' names in these early published versions indicates that the text for these plays came from Shakespeare's own manuscript. A stage manager or a transcriber would have standardized the names of the characters.

Building theatres outside of London meant that the companies were free of City ordinances, and several theatres, including the Globe, would later be built across the river in Southwark for this reason. The plays were still subject to State statutes, and the Act for the Punishment of Vagabonds of 1572 required all greater London companies to have royal, noble, or judicial patronage, in part as a means of controlling the content of their plays. Shakespeare ran afoul of the censors with *Richard II*, after Essex's failed attempt to depose the Queen. Elizabeth is supposed to have said, "I am Richard II," and so its abdication scene did not appear in published versions of the play until the last of its four quartos and the Folio, both published after her death in 1601.

Contents

The introduction to the Folio also contains a table of contents that divides its plays into comedies, histories and tragedies. As the Folio was printed after Shakespeare's death, we should question whether he thought of his plays in those terms.

Shakespeare wrote to existing forms early in his career, as playwrights often do. *The Comedy of Errors* and *Titus Andronicus* are modeled after ancient Roman comedies and tragedies, which were being rediscovered at this time, but is *Romeo and Juliet* a tragedy, as listed in the Folio? The play is arguably a comedy until Mercutio's death. Conversely, the first act of the "comedy," *As You Like It*, is not predominantly comedic in tone. Orlando is tossed out of his home; Rosalind is sent into exile by her uncle, the usurping Duke. Productions that try to force the humor here can flounder.

Shakespeare experimented with form throughout his long career, and we must be wary of generic labels for his plays and let what is on the page lead us to discover their genres. His preoccupation with leadership in his histories gradually morphed into his tragedies, where the comedic scenes of the histories become a key component of *Macbeth*, among others. *Julius Caesar* is a transitional play – a history that turns into a tragedy halfway through. Shakespeare's comedies, which often have disturbing episodes such as Malvolio's imprisonment in *Twelfth Night*, evolved into what we now call the problem plays because the comedy becomes so dark. The Folio has a difficult time in squeezing the later so-called romances into the three categories: *The Tempest* is listed as a comedy in the Folio, while *Cymbeline* is listed as a tragedy.

It is also important to note what the Folio does not contain. Scene locations were added by subsequent editors beginning with Nicholas Rowe, who assembled the first collected edition to follow the folios in 1709.[7] Shakespeare wrote for a fluid stage, where locations need to change instantly and explicit settings get in the way. When he wished to, he created locations with the spoken word. Most contemporary editions now eliminate scene locations, but still include character listings, although only six exist in the Folio and none in the quartos. The terminology they contain may distort Shakespeare's intentions. Designations such as *Lord* and *Lady* Capulet can be, as we will see, misleading.

Most but not all of the Folio plays are divided into acts; only half have scene divisions. The quartos have neither of these. *Macbeth*, for one, does seem to fall into the five-act model of the Senecan tragedies, but some of his plays are more fluid. Act divisions may lead us to assume that a play peaks at the end of an act that was not even Shakespeare's conception.

Quartos

The Prologue to *Romeo and Juliet* discussed in Chapter 1 was not printed in the Folio. It comes from an earlier single-play edition called a quarto. *Quartos* were so named because paper was folded into *quarters* for binding. It produced a book of smaller dimensions, and at sixpence a much less expensive one than the Folio.

Half of the Folio plays were published in earlier quartos from 1594 to the publication of the First Folio in 1623. Ten of these eighteen plays were sold and printed between 1597 and 1600, when the company was raising cash to pay for the construction of their new theatre. The Globe opened in 1599 on the south side of the Thames outside the City limits near the Rose, the theatre of their principal rivals, the Admiral's Men. In this neighborhood, theatre competed with bear-baiting arenas for entertainment.

The list of plays first printed in quartos leaves the impression that they were among Shakespeare's hits. The great cycle of English history plays helped make his reputation as a playwright.[8] *Romeo and Juliet*, *Hamlet*, *Othello,* and *Lear* are still among the most popular of his plays today. The other tragedy published in quarto, *Titus Andronicus*, was an early success. *A Midsummer Nights' Dream* and *Much Ado About Nothing* are among the most produced of his comedies today; *The Merry Wives of Windsor* fed Elizabethan audiences' hunger for the character of Falstaff. *The Merchant of Venice*, *Love's Labour's Lost*, and *Troilus and Cressida* complete the list.

Bill Bryson writes that, of the 3,000 or so plays staged in the seventy-five years before the closure of the theatres in 1642, "only 230 or so play texts still exist . . . including the thirty-eight by Shakespeare . . . a gloriously staggering proportion."[9]

The First Quarto of *Romeo* is a pirated edition. Printing a play had serious implications. Anyone could publish a play, or what they purported was the play, if they registered a "copy" with the London Company of Stationers. Once published, any theatre company could produce them. For this reason, theatre companies protected copies of their plays and did not sell them to publishers until they no longer frequented their repertory. Actors received only sides for their scenes, including bit players who were not part of the permanent acting company and did not share in its profits.

Some of these sides found their way into what we call today "bad quartos." Heminges and Condell state in the second of their introductions to the Folio that it was published in part to preserve Shakespeare's plays as he conceived them, "as where (before) you were abus'd with diuerse stolne, and surreptitious copies, maimed, and deformed by the frauds and stealthes of iniurious impostors."[10] Where did these bad quartos come from? The First Quarto of *Hamlet* (1603) most closely resembles subsequent printings of the play when the minor characters of Marcellus and the First Player are onstage.[11] The actors (or actor if these roles doubled) who played these parts may have recited their lines to a transcriber or sold their sides to a publisher who was trying to beat Shakespeare's company to publication of a popular play. Other parts of the play would have been reconstructed from memory or from stenography during performance. Thomas Heywood complained that his plays had been published without his consent and were "so corrupt and mangled (coppied onley by the eare) that I have been . . . ashamed to challenge them."[12]

The results in the First Quarto of *Hamlet* are sometimes hilarious. These are Q1's opening lines of Hamlet's most famous soliloquy. Capital "I" could mean "ay" at this time:

> To be, or not to be, I [ay] there's the point,
> To Die, to sleepe, is that all? I [ay] all:
> No, to sleepe, to dreame, I mary [ay, marry] there it goes . . .

The First Quarto of *Romeo and Juliet* (1597) has the hallmarks of a bad quarto. Its text is less corrupt than Q1 of *Hamlet*, but contains "recollections, transpositions, paraphrases, summaries, repetitions and omissions of words, phrases or lines correctly presented in Q2."[13] One reason bad quartos can still be useful today is because of the visual stage directions some contain. After all, they are in part records of someone watching the play and may provide details of the original staging, such as: "They all but the Nurse goe foorth, casting Rosemary on her [Juliet's body] and shutting the Curtens."[14] This may have provided the cover to remove the "dead" Juliet and her bed, while the musicians' scene proceeded without interruption.

The title page of the Q2 of *Romeo* (1599) states that it is "Newly corrected, augmented and amended," a reference to the previous bad quarto. It is about 800 lines longer than Q1. The Second Quarto is now considered the authoritative version of the play because the Folio version of *Romeo and Juliet* was reprinted from the third and fourth quartos, which are themselves reprints of earlier quartos. With each subsequent edition, printing errors were compounded and changes would be made when there was a perceived problem in the text.

Folio or quarto?

In addition to the eighteen plays published in Folio for the first time, the Folio supersedes the text for four plays that only exist in bad quartos: 2–3 *Henry VI, Henry V*, and *The Merry Wives of Windsor*. For these twenty-two plays, the Folio is the authoritative source.

Nine of the canonical plays[15] in the folios, including *Romeo and Juliet* and *Pericles*, are reprints from quartos. For these a quarto is the authoritative text, although the Folio adds important scenes for two of these plays – the banquet scene in *Titus Andronicus* and the abdication scene in *Richard II* that was discussed earlier in this chapter.

For the remaining six plays, however – *Richard III*, *2 Henry IV, Troilus and Cressida*, *Hamlet*, *Lear,* and *Othello* – the quarto and Folio texts differ more substantially. This is not surprising. As those who work on contemporary plays know, theatre scripts exist in different versions: multiple drafts from the author, revisions and cuts made during rehearsals, and published versions. Scholars have deduced that author's manuscript and prompt-book copy were the main sources for the original publications of Shakespeare's plays. Shakespeare's manuscript copy is considered the closest to his intentions, but often has problems because of illegibility and omissions: Shakespeare did not always indicate exits, for example. In the first tavern scene in *1 Henry IV*, Mistress Quickly's exit to answer the knocking at the door looks fine on the page, but doesn't work when you put the play on its feet. There are too few lines to cover her exit and return with the sheriff. We found the exit a few pages earlier, and got a laugh to boot.[16]

Editors also deduce manuscript copy when there are inconsistencies that the book-keeper would have standardized for rehearsal. In Q2 of *Romeo and Juliet*, Peter is called both Clown and Kemp, the actor who played him. This is one reason why it is believed that the Second Quarto of *Romeo and Juliet* comes from the author's manuscript and is preferred as closest to Shakespeare's original intentions. Scholars believe that about half of the Folio versions of Shakespeare's plays were derived from handwritten manuscript copy.

In Shakespeare's time, the book-keeper kept a prompt book that would be a cleaner copy than the author's manuscript. These scripts would have contained revisions and cuts made during rehearsal or performance, and sometimes prior to it by a censor. For these reasons, prompt-book copy *sometimes* takes precedence over manuscript copy. *Macbeth* is an unusually short play and may contain cuts. It is free of inconsistencies in designations and contains what look like sound cues for performance. For all these reasons it is deduced that the only version we have of this play comes from prompt-book copy.

Earlier published editions and transcriptions were also used for publication. One quarto begot the next and sometimes was the source text for the Folio. In addition, scribes were sometimes paid to produce clean transcriptions for archival purposes or to submit to the censor. All plays had to be licensed by the Master of the Revels, who could censor a play, as he did with *Richard II*. Gary Taylor has posited that the quarto of *Henry V* was probably a touring version for a smaller cast.[17] Touring was important for London theatre companies for income during the off-season and during plague years when the London theatres were shut down. As a touring version of the play, this is an example of a quarto that, although published first, represents a later version of the play than that in the Folio of 1623, which was set from manuscript copy.

To collate or not to collate

With few exceptions, contemporary editions collate the plays that have existing quartos with their Folio counterparts. The six plays that have seriously competing texts present the greatest challenge, and we should examine their choices if something seems wrong. If it can be deduced that one version comes from the author's manuscript, that usually takes precedence. But what is a final script in a medium as fluid as theatre? Is the last version the best representation of a play? Did Shakespeare always agree with the cuts that were made? Bertolt Brecht continued to revise many of his plays throughout his life, and some revisions are not as strong as their earlier versions.

Hamlet is a particularly thorny problem. Shakespeare seems to have struggled with a play that was a leap forward for him, particularly in his mastery of the soliloquy to suggest interior thoughts. The Second Quarto and Folio editions of *Hamlet* contain many differences, and *each* has passages not found in the other. Some contemporary editors believe that these versions represent such fundamentally different ideas about the play that collating the Q2 and Folio texts will only muddy the text. The Arden Press recently published both versions for this reason.

Notes

1 Produced by the Public Theater in New York's Central Park in 2013.
2 *The Norton Facsimile: The First Folio of Shakespeare*, ed. Charlton Hinman (Norton, 1968), p. x.
3 Ibid., p. 6.
4 Andrew Gurr, *The Shakespearean Stage, 1574–1642* (Cambridge, 1980), pp. 45–46. An excellent history of the development of Elizabethan theatres.
5 Gary Taylor, *Reinventing Shakespeare* (Weidenfeld & Nicolson, 1989), p. 25.
6 *The Norton Facsimile: The First Folio of Shakespeare*, ed. Hinman, p. 17.
7 New collected editions followed every 20 years or so in the 1700s by editors whose names still appear in collation notes today. The Cambridge series in the 1860s moved away from the practice of a single editor for all plays.
8 The first of these histories, *1 Henry VI*, was not printed in quarto.
9 Bill Bryson, *Shakespeare: The World as Stage* (Atlas, 2007), pp. 18–19.
10 *The Norton Facsimile: The First Folio of Shakespeare*, ed. Hinman, p. 7.
11 *Shakespeare's Plays in Quarto*, eds. Michael J. B. Allen and Kenneth Muir (University of California Press, 1981), p. xiv. This compilation of quartos is an extraordinary resource for checking the text of contemporary editions.
12 Ibid., p. xiii.
13 *Romeo and Juliet*, ed. Brian Gibbons, Arden Second Series (Methuen, 1980), Introduction p. 2.
14 *Shakespeare's Plays in Quarto*, eds. Allen and Muir, p. 150.
15 Two other plays thought to be collaborations are now published in Arden Shakespeare editions. It is believed that Shakespeare played a smaller role in the writing of *The Two Noble Kinsmen*; *Double Falsehood* is a more recent candidate for co-authorship.

16 *Henry IV, Part One*, ed. A. R. Humphreys, Arden Second Series (Methuen, 1960), 2.4. Most editions indicate the exit at line 475; we moved it earlier to lines 390–91. Directed by Des McAnuff, New York Shakespeare Festival, 1982.
17 *Henry V*, ed. Gary Taylor (Oxford World Classics, 1982), p. 22.

Bibliography

Shakespeare editions cited

Henry IV, Part One. Ed. A. R. Humphreys, Arden Second Series. Methuen, 1960.
Henry V. Ed. Gary Taylor. Oxford World Classics, 1982.
The Norton Facsimile: The First Folio of Shakespeare. Ed. Charlton Hinman. Norton, 1968.
Romeo and Juliet. Ed. Brian Gibbons, Arden Second Series. Methuen, 1980.
Shakespeare's Plays in Quarto. Eds. Michael J. B. Allen and Kenneth Muir. University of California Press, 1981.

Other sources

Bryson, Bill. *Shakespeare: The World as Stage*. Atlas Books, 2007.
Gurr, Andrew. *The Shakespearean Stage, 1574–1642*. Cambridge, 1980.
Taylor, Gary. *Reinventing Shakespeare*. Weidenfeld & Nicolson, 1989.

3 Juliet and Romeo

In this and the next chapters I want to focus on the private story outlined in the Prologue: "the passage of their death-marked love." Passage is an active word: it implies a journey, and that journey can be charted by Romeo and Juliet's use of language. My focus will turn from Shakespeare's choice of words to their arrangement into verse and prose and how Shakespeare uses poetry to create characterizations. There is a tendency in writing about this play to lump the title characters together, to talk about them as if they are the same people on the same journey. Shakespeare uses elementary playwriting tools to differentiate them right at the beginning. Romeo speaks almost nonstop in his first scene. Shakespeare introduces Juliet in a scene of some 105 lines and she speaks only seven of them.

"Where's my daughter?"

Shakespeare begins to characterize Juliet even before she enters. She has already been called into her mother's presence, but it takes several more entreaties from the Nurse to get her onstage. Her mother dismisses the Nurse so that she and Juliet can "talk in secret,"[1] but changes her mind. Perhaps she will have a better chance to persuade Juliet with the Nurse present. That turns out to be a miscalculation. It becomes clear that Juliet is closer to the Nurse than to her mother, and the Nurse is not afraid to take advantage of that. Her mother states that Juliet is not yet fourteen; the Nurse does her one better with, "Faith, I can tell her age unto an hour."[2] We know that this is a challenge because she begins the line with a mild swear word.

The Nurse is often presented solely as comic relief. This robs working-class characters of their point of view. The Nurse is accurate in her description of Juliet as a strong and willful child, who even as a baby could throw a tantrum that could, in the Nurse's eyes, shake the house. Her mother twice tries to silence the Nurse, but it takes Juliet to get her to shut up. Her mother now brings up the subject of marriage, for Paris will be present at the ball. Note how ambiguous Juliet is in her response to her mother's question:

CAPULET'S WIFE
How stands your disposition to be married?
JULIET
It is an honour that I dream not of.[3]

The Nurse's comments on Paris can also be understood in two ways:

NURSE
A man, young lady, lady, such a man
As all the world – why, he's a man of wax.[4]

"A man of wax" may mean a perfectly molded man, or (perhaps because of this) someone who is perfectly dull. These dual meanings allow the Nurse to insinuate without openly opposing her mistress. After Mercutio's death, the Nurse will add her voice to those urging Juliet to marry Paris. If she does not support Paris here, her later turnaround will leave Juliet with a greater sense of betrayal. Making the choice that allows for the greater journey increases the dramatic stakes in a play.

Juliet's mother now delivers a sixteen-line verse homily that is a favorite passage of mine. The eighteenth-century poet and Shakespeare editor Alexander Pope called it "a ridiculous speech,"[5] but that is rarely acknowledged in production today. Four hundred years separate us from the language of Shakespeare's plays, and it is sometimes difficult today to hear the nuance in that language. Verse in Shakespeare need not always be good poetry. What seems arch and self-conscious in Romeo's verse is part of Shakespeare's characterization of him. What seems stiff and awkward in Juliet's mother's speech here is Shakespeare's way of characterizing her. She now compares Paris to a book, not the right image to attract a young girl. The rattling of the singsong rhymed couplets underlines the banality of what she says, and note how she gets lost in her imagery halfway through her speech:

> This precious book of love [Paris], this unbound lover,
> To beautify him only lacks a cover [Juliet].
> The fish lives in the sea, and 'tis much pride
> For fair without the fair within to hide.
> That book in many's eyes doth share the glory
> That in *gold* clasps locks in the *golden* story. [italics added][6]

Where the image of the fish in the sea comes from is something that only Juliet's mother knows. When she returns to the book image, it is so contorted that it is almost incoherent. Shakespeare gilds her verse, literally, to infer Paris's wealth *and* reveal her interest in it. Jill Levenson states that "Capulet's wife views the match as a social and economic coup as well as a fulfilling romance."[7] Social status again enters the play. Capulet's wife uses the word "gold" as an image of delight. Later, Romeo will give that word a darker meaning.

Juliet's response to her mother's lengthy entreaty is cleverly crafted. The beginning of her line is direct, but tempered in its *seeming* agreeability by what follows:

CAPULET'S WIFE
. . . can you like of Paris' love?
JULIET
I'll look to like, if looking liking move,
But no more deep will I indart mine eye
Than your consent gives strength to make it fly.[8]

At the end of the scene a servant tells her mother that "the guests are come, supper served up, you called, my young lady asked for, the Nurse cursed in the pantry, and everything in extremity."[9] Juliet's mother is not in control of the Nurse, her daughter, or her household. This picture of the Capulet household in disarray will continue throughout the play and parallels the disarray in Verona caused by the two families.

The sonnet

Scholars believe that *Romeo and Juliet* was written during a period when Shakespeare took a stunning leap into high poetry with *Romeo*, *Love's Labour's Lost*, and *Richard II*. Perhaps this was influenced by the poems he wrote when London theatres were closed during the plague years of 1592–3. The long narrative poem *Venus and Adonis* was "far more successful in print than any of his plays."[10] Dympna Callaghan points out the "stylistic affinities" of his love sonnets with *Romeo and Juliet*, which "was written at the height of the sonnet vogue [in England]."[11]

The English sonnet was a poem of fourteen lines with a logical structure, usually built on quatrains and enforced by a strict rhyme scheme. A *volta* or turn in thought in the final couplet brings the sonnet to its conclusion. A sonnet introduces each of the play's first two acts. When Romeo and Juliet first meet, they also share a sonnet – with an extra quatrain added at the end. Romeo makes the first move. He touches Juliet, as indicated in his lines, and is relentless in persuading her to accept a kiss. For her part, Juliet is his match in fielding his advances – until she changes her mind in the first line of the volta [italicized below] in the concluding couplet:

ROMEO
If I profane with my unworthiest hand a
This holy shrine, the gentle sin is this, b
My lips, two blushing pilgrims, ready stand a
To smooth that rough touch with a tender kiss. b
JULIET
Good pilgrim, you do wrong your hand too much, c
Which mannerly devotion shows in this, b
For saints have hands that pilgrims' hands do touch, c
And palm to palm is holy palmers' kiss. b
ROMEO
Have not saints lips, and holy palmers too? d
JULIET
Ay, pilgrim, lips that they must use in prayer. e
ROMEO
O then, dear saint, let lips do what hands do; d
They pray, grant thou, lest faith turn to despair. e
JULIET
Saints do not move, but grant for prayer's sake f
ROMEO
Then move not while my prayer's effect I take. f
He kisses her
ROMEO
Thus from my lips, by thine, my sin is purged. g
JULIET
Then have my lips the sin that they have took. h
ROMEO
Sin from my lips? O trcspass sweetly urged! g
Give me my sin again.
He kisses her
JULIET You kiss by th'book.[12] h

Sharing the sonnet binds their dialogue in our hearing of it. After their opening quatrains, they start sharing rhymes to emphasize the growth in connection. He kisses her at the end of the sonnet and, in the extra quatrain, they share the last verse line to seal that connection. Juliet ends the passage with a bit of humor. "By the book" can imply either well done or stiffly done by rote, and the actor has a legitimate choice either way. Unlike Lady Capulet's speech, which is written entirely in rhymed couplets, the alternating rhymes of the quatrains don't jangle in our ears. They give the dialogue a sense of the pleasure both Juliet and Romeo take from their repartee.

The balcony scene

Romeo and Juliet next meet in the balcony scene, and it is here that Shakespeare most clearly differentiates the young lovers, as they exist at the beginning of the play, through language. Note how Juliet speaks in simple words with little adornment:

JULIET
'Tis but thy name that is my enemy;
Thou art thyself, though not a Montague.
What's Montague? It is nor hand nor foot,
Nor arm nor face, nor any other part
Belonging to a man. O be some other name!
What's in a name? That which we call a rose
By any other word would smell as sweet;
So Romeo would, were he not Romeo called,
Retain that dear perfection which he owes
Without that title. Romeo, doff thy name,
And for thy name, which is no part of thee,
Take all myself.
ROMEO
I take thee at thy word.[13]

This speech contains few adjectives and only one beautiful image – that of a rose – and ends with a call to arms. Yet it is glorious poetry. Q2–4 and the Folio use the phrase "by any other *word*"; the bad quarto, Q1, substitutes "by any other name." The latter was used by Alexander Pope, the eighteenth-century poet and an early editor of Shakespeare's plays. Many subsequent editors have followed his lead; you may have heard it in productions. Brian Gibbons in his Arden edition argues that Shakespeare goes back and forth between "name" and "word," making a distinction in their use, and that there is no need to substitute "name" for "word" here.[14] This distinction helps to make Romeo's conclusion clearer: he implies that he will doff his name, Montague, at her request, as it is her "enemy," and take her "at [her] word" instead.

Romeo, by contrast, is a man of words and talks in the overheated and voluble style of a Petrarchan lover: Juliet is the sun, bright angel, dear saint. Petrarch was the Italian poet who popularized the love sonnet. Juliet asks Romeo to doff his name; Romeo asks her, as he did with Rosaline, to cast off her virginity:

Arise, fair sun, and kill the envious moon,
Who is already sick and pale with grief
That thou, her maid, art far more fair than she.

Be not her maid, since she is envious;
Her vestal[15] livery is but sick and green
And none but fools do wear it. Cast it off.[16]

Romeo's opening lines are justly famous and moving in their youthful exuberance. However, his personification of Juliet as the sun who will outshine the envious, virginal moon – Rosaline – goes on for a full nine lines. His poetry lacks the simplicity of Juliet's verse, and he eventually becomes trapped by his verbosity into the overwrought image that concludes his opening speech:

Two of the fairest stars in all the heaven,
Having some business, do entreat her eyes
To twinkle in their spheres till they return.
What if her eyes were there, they in her head?
The brightness of her cheek would shame those stars
As daylight doth a lamp; her eye in heaven
Would through the airy regions stream so bright
That birds would sing and think it were not night.[17]

After comparing Juliet to the sun, he next calls her "bright angel." Further on, she becomes "dear saint." His hyperbolic words can be quite a mouthful. Shakespeare deliberately withholds a place to pause in the last five verse lines below to show how overblown they are. See what happens when you try to say this speech in one breath:

O speak again, bright angel, for thou art
As glorious to this night, being o'er my head,
As is a wingèd[18] messenger of heaven
Unto the white-upturnèd wond'ring eyes
Of mortals that fall back to gaze on him
When he bestrides the lazy-puffing clouds
And sails upon the bosom of the air.[19]

Shakespeare uses Romeo's verbosity to comic effect, and his exuberance gives this scene a comedic tone that is generally accepted today, but which was taken more seriously by the Victorians who considered his verse exemplary poetry. Later in this scene, Shakespeare uses alliteration [italics added] to underline the artificiality of Romeo's poetry; by this time even Juliet has had enough. She stops him twice to prevent him from speaking further:

ROMEO
Lady, by yonder blessèd moon I vow,
That *tips* with silver all these *fruit-tree tops* –

JULIET

O swear not by the moon, th'inconstant moon,
That monthly changes in her circled orb,
Lest thy love prove likewise variable.

ROMEO

What shall I swear by?

JULIET

Do not swear at all;
Or if thou wilt, swear by thy gracious self,
Which is the god of my idolatry,
And I'll believe thee.

ROMEO

If my heart's dear love –

JULIET

Well, do not swear. Although I joy in thee,
I have no joy in this contract tonight:
It is too rash, too unadvised, too sudden . . .[20]

As with Sampson and Gregory, the difference between the characters here creates the tension in the scene and gives it shape. Romeo is a man of words; Juliet is a woman of action. Her first words in this scene are a call to action:

Deny thy father and refuse thy name;
Or if thou wilt not, be but sworn my love,
And I'll no longer be a Capulet.[21]

She goes a step further at the end of the scene:

If that thy bent of love be honorable,
Thy purpose marriage, send me word tomorrow,
By one that I'll procure to come to thee . . .
And all my fortunes at thy foot I'll lay,
And follow thee, my lord, throughout the world.[22]

In between she has some of the most beautiful poetry in Shakespeare. Few lines here or elsewhere can match these:

My bounty is as boundless as the sea,
My love as deep; the more I give to thee,
The more I have, for both are infinite.[23]

It is Juliet who is the great poet of Shakespeare's play. Even Romeo acknowledges this when next they meet to be married: ". . . that thy skill be more to blazon it."[24] Her poetry points the way to Shakespeare's more mature style of verse. With Romeo, Shakespeare is deliberately using self-conscious artifice to characterize and qualify this young man – and not without sympathy. We all have been young and full of ourselves and have flashed our peacock feathers. Perhaps the artifice of a character like Romeo is Shakespeare's way of saying goodbye to his current style of verse writing. He will experiment with more prose in the plays that follow, the two parts of *Henry IV* and his series of great comedies – *As You Like It, Much Ado About Nothing,* and *Twelfth Night*. When he returns to tragedy a more mature use of verse will emerge, one that we will examine in *Macbeth*.

Romeo's encounter with Juliet will gradually change them both. As he tells the Friar in the next scene, "my heart's dear love is set / On the fair daughter of rich Capulet. / As mine on hers, *so hers is set on mine*. [Italics added]"[25] Romeo is experiencing the power of reciprocal love, something he did not have with Rosaline and something that is usually overlooked in the simplified, romantic notions about love at first sight. Sentimentalizing Shakespeare obscures the full beauty of his observations. Reciprocal love is important in Shakespeare's canon. Its presence and lack is contrasted in another play written in this period – *A Midsummer Night's Dream* – and in many that will follow. The use of analogs in other plays of Shakespeare will be further examined in the second half of this book.

When they next meet just before the marriage ceremony, Juliet yet again reminds Romeo that "Conceit, more rich in matter than in words, / Brags of his substance, not of ornament."[26] We are still at the beginning of their journey, however. They are two distinct characters, and they go on different journeys and those journeys will continue to be charted by their use of language.

The point of no return

What's in a word? The good intentions of Romeo, Benvolio, the Friar, and the Nurse lead nowhere in this play full of remarkable words because words are not sufficient to stop the violence. Romeo is dragged into the feud in the middle of the play when the kind of skirmish we saw at the beginning reoccurs and he kills Tybalt. Neither his fate nor Juliet's, however, is yet sealed. This is a turning point in the play, but not I think the point of no return. After he kills Tybalt, Romeo is exiled. He and Juliet have their farewell scene together, and then the short Act Four focuses on her. When we next see Romeo in exile at the top of Act Five, he speaks with calm authority:

> If I may trust the flattering truth of sleep,
> My dreams presage some joyful news at hand.
> My bosom's lord [his heart] sits lightly in his throne,
> And all this day an unaccustomed spirit

Lifts me above the ground with cheerful thoughts.
I dreamt my lady came and found me dead –
Strange dream that gives a dead man leave to think! –
And breathed such life with kisses in my lips
That I revived and was an emperor.[27]

This is a new Romeo and his language tells us that. Away from the poisonous atmosphere of Verona, he has benefited from sleep, something he and others have lacked. His verse here is simple and eloquent. The change in his language shows just how far the experience of a reciprocal love has transformed him. This beautiful vision, in which Juliet's kisses bring him back to life, is his best poetry in the play.

Unfortunately, he hears the false news that Juliet is dead and that sends him back to Verona, where he makes a critical mistake. Shakespeare adds a scene that is not in the source material. The point of no return is frequently glossed over in productions that trivialize Paris and cast an unappealing actor in that role. His death is even cut from some stage and film versions. Prior to Paris' death, it is conceivable that the Friar's plan will work and that the lovers can escape the poisonous atmosphere in Verona as they planned. We can understand Romeo's outrage at Tybalt for killing his friend, if not condone his actions. Paris, however, is there to mourn Juliet and believes that Romeo is there to desecrate her tomb. There can be no happy ending to *Romeo and Juliet* after Romeo kills Paris.

The play has more than once described the combustible nature of young love in imagery that literally uses gunpowder. Indeed, both Romeo and Juliet try to commit suicide in scenes with the Friar that follow Mercutio and Tybalt's deaths. Shakespeare shows us how their understandable impetuosity is one of the multiple components that contribute to "their death-marked love." Romeo, however, bears additional responsibility. He could have walked away from Paris, but that is not who he is – or is it rather what this young man has become? Shakespeare lets us decide, but the latter choice gives him a greater journey in the play.

And so, Romeo succumbs to violence for a *second* time and seals their fate. He kills Paris and enters the tomb, says goodbye to Juliet with a lengthy speech that betrays the language of the old Romeo, and kills himself.

Juliet's journey

Romeo is defined in the context of a competitive world of male posturing and violence. At the end of Act Three, Shakespeare passes the focus to Juliet for an entire act that follows her in the context of her family. That should tell us that there is another component to "their death-marked love." Marriage to Paris becomes a necessity after Tybalt, a Capulet, slays Mercutio, a kinsman to the Prince. Despite Capulet's love for his daughter, Juliet becomes fair game and she is pulled into the public story by the need of her family to shore up their relationship to the Prince. This time Capulet and his wife quickly agree to Paris' suit – and in Act Four Juliet is put through a crucible that parallels Romeo's in Act Three.

What a resilient character this fourteen-year old girl is! When the Nurse turns on Romeo in the "Gallop apace" scene, Juliet leaps to his defense. When her parents insist that she marry Paris, she refuses to consider it. After the Friar hatches his plan, Juliet conceals her true feelings to her parents and even deceives her confidant, the Nurse. When she tells Juliet to marry Paris, even though she is already married, Juliet calls her "Ancient damnation."[28] Juliet is truly alone for the long monologue in which she drinks the sleeping potion. It contains a verbosity that we have rarely heard from her. Have circumstances destroyed the most magnificent character in the play?

In the tomb scene, Juliet awakens and finds Romeo dead. "Thy lips are warm" is spoken when she realizes that Romeo has just died. These are the saddest words in this sad play.[29] Juliet remains true to her nature and kills herself at the end of ten lines.

Notes

1 *Romeo and Juliet*, ed. Jill L. Levenson (Oxford World's Classics, 2000), 1.3.9.
2 Ibid., 1.3.12. *Faith* is short for, in Faith or by my Faith.
3 Ibid., 1.3.67–68.
4 Ibid., 1.3.77–78.
5 Ibid., note on lines 1.3.81–96: Pope misses the point here and cuts the speech.
6 Ibid., 1.3.89–94.
7 Ibid., note on 1.3.94.
8 Ibid., 1.3.98–101.
9 Ibid., 1.3.102–4.
10 Bill Bryson, *Shakespeare: The World as Stage* (Atlas Books, 2007), p. 88.
11 *Romeo and Juliet*, ed. Dympna Callaghan (Bedford/St. Martin's, 2003), p. 11.
12 *Romeo and Juliet*, ed. Levenson, 1.4.206–23.
13 Ibid., 2.1.81–92.
14 *Romeo and Juliet*, ed. Brian Gibbons, Arden Second Edition (Methuen, 1980), note on 2.2.44.
15 The vestal virgins of ancient Rome were associated with the goddess Diana, personified by the moon.
16 *Romeo and Juliet*, ed. Levenson, 2.1.47–52.
17 Ibid., 2.1.58–65.
18 This Oxford edition uses an accent over the "e" in words ending in "-èd", *if* the "e" is to be sounded. Conversely, the Arden editions quoted in my book contract the last syllable as "'d", when words ending in "-ed" are not to be sounded.
19 Ibid., 2.1.69–75.
20 Ibid., 2.1.150–61.
21 Ibid., 2.1.77–79.
22 Ibid., 2.1.186–91.

23 Ibid., 2.1.176–78.
24 Ibid., 2.5.25–6.
25 Ibid., 2.2.57–59.
26 Ibid., 2.5.30–31.
27 Ibid., 5.1.1–9.
28 Ibid., 3.5.235.
29 Ibid., 5.3.167.

Bibliography

Shakespeare editions cited

Romeo and Juliet. Ed. Brian Gibbons, Arden Second Series. Methuen,1980.
Romeo and Juliet. Ed. Dympna Callaghan. Bedford/St. Martin's, 2003.
Romeo and Juliet. Ed. Jill L. Levenson. Oxford World's Classics, 2000.

Other source

Bryson, Bill. *Shakespeare: The World as Stage*. Atlas Books, 2007.

4 The aural word

Verse and prose

What is the nature of stage language, its essentials? Theatre is an aural medium, and it moves forward in time. We cannot go back and reread a passage we didn't understand the first time around. For this reason, Shakespeare often gives us critical pieces of information more than once. And he uses verse and rhetoric, standard at the time, to help us *hear* that information clearly. They are natural aids in an aural medium, and if we approach them with this in mind, it is easier to understand why they are used and what that can tell us about the text.

Verse

Verse was the medium for imaginative writing for thousands of years because literature was made for public recitation before the invention of printing. The type of verse that Shakespeare used – blank verse – was introduced around 1540 in Lord Surrey's translation of Virgil's *Aeneid*. In English we tend to alternate accented and unaccented syllables, and the iambic pentameter of blank verse simply regularizes the way we construct our sentences. Because of this, iambic pentameter makes dialogue easier to speak rapidly, because if we say two accented syllables in sequence we need to put a pause in between. It also makes it easier to hear because it is easier to focus on the melody, that is, the words, when the rhythm is constant.

The line that follows is in iambic pentameter – two syllables to a foot, the accented syllable second, and five feet to a line:

```
 -   /     -   /    -    /     -    /      -   /  (-)
An i'mb | is just | the way | we speak | in English.
```

In English, we put the modifier before the emphasized noun; verbs are often followed by an emphasized adverb. Pronouns usually precede the emphasized verb; prepositions introduce their emphasized object. Pentameter is closer to the way we phrase thoughts in English than, for example, the more verbose French. Their verse line is six feet long and in trochees, two syllables to a foot, with the accented syllable *first*, because in French, the order of words differs: the modifier, for example, follows the emphasized noun, the reverse of English.

The example above displays two frequent variants in blank verse. "Iamb" must be contracted to make it a regular blank verse line. Contractions can be a challenge in performing Shakespeare because some words were contracted differently in Elizabethan English. In the same sentence, the extra, unaccented syllable at the end is called a feminine ending. It can occur at the end of verse line, sentence, or clause and occasionally even a phrase. That means it may appear in the middle of a verse line if that is where a sentence or clause ends. Another frequent variant is the trochee. It reverses the stress of an iambic foot and usually occurs at the *beginning* of a line, sentence, or clause.

These rhythmic changes not only provide vocal variety, but also help organize a line *aurally* so that its sense is clearer. The change in rhythm that a trochee provides can signal a change in thought. A trochee at the beginning of a verse line or sentence that has a feminine ending can help us hear that line as a unit of thought. In these instances, they perform the function that punctuation does in a print medium.

Because of the extra syllable, multiple feminine endings slow down verse and may give a scene a languorous feeling. They are sometimes used to help create a mood of formal politeness, as when Lady Macbeth welcomes Duncan into her castle. Given what we know about her intentions, her gracious formality here only underlines her insincerity.

A series of trochees can add a drive or an agitated state to a scene. Take this oft-cited example where Juliet orders the sun god to race his chariot to sunset in the west, so she can meet with Romeo under the cloak of night. I have underlined the series of trochees that begin many of the lines and clauses. The pace of the passage is also increased by the number of contractions (italics added below) that are needed to maintain the scansion, as well as the repeated use of the word "come" at the end. The latter is a rhetorical figure we will discuss in the next chapter:

Gallop apace, you fiery-footed steeds,
Towards [*Tords*] Phoebus' lodging. Such a wagoner
As Phaëton would whip you to the west,
And bring in cloudy night immediately [*im-med'-yat-ly'*].
Spread thy close curtain, love-performing night,
That runaways' [*run' -ways*] eyes may wink, and Romeo [*3 syllables*]
Leap to these arms, untalked of and unseen.
Lovers can see to do their amorous [*am'-rous*] rites
By their own beauties …
Come night, come Romeo [*Rom'-yo*], come thou day in night;

For thou wilt lie upon the wings of night
Whiter than new snow upon a raven's back.
Come gentle night, come loving black-browed night,
Give me my Romeo [*Rom'-yo*]; and when I shall die,
Take him and cut him out in little stars…[1]

This speech demonstrates some of the variations Shakespeare used to maintain or break the scansion of blank verse. "Romeo" can be two or three syllables, depending on which is needed to scan the line; the same is true of the word "Juliet" in other passages. The vowel in the last syllable of "untalked" was dropped then as it is now.[2] Note that in some instances – "come Romeo" is one example – the syllables can be scanned as iambs or trochees, determined by which word the actor wishes to emphasize. Finally, the line that begins, "Whiter than new snow upon a raven's back," has an extra syllable in it. Some editors drop the word "new," or change "upon" to "on," to make the line scan, following "corrections" that the compositors of the Fourth Quarto and Second Folio made. Many editors, including Levenson, keep the line intact, and I think they are right to do so. Shakespeare was a rule breaker, and his use of verse would become increasingly free in his later plays.

Later in this scene, Juliet sounds the -ed in "banishèd" in order to make those lines scan. Our Juliet in the La Jolla production – Amanda Plummer – felt that repeatedly voicing that last syllable sounded too artificial today.[3] Instead, she said "banish'd" but followed it with a brief pause to keep the iambic rhythm of the line. It worked in part because the pause emphasized the importance of that word to the speech.

Iambic pentameter appears in surprising places today. David Mamet experimented with it in *American Buffalo*.[4] The regularity of the meter is one reason his dialogue has such vigor. Mamet also inserted pauses to maintain regular scansion. Pauses are a frequent device in contemporary drama: Pinter and Becket do it as well. Shakespeare *may* indicate pauses by using a short verse line, that is, an incomplete line of pentameter that is filled out by a pause or an action, such as an exit. In the speech of the Bleeding Captain at the beginning of *Macbeth*, his short lines seem to indicate pauses for the wounded man to catch his breath. Filling out short lines with pauses for actions is still a matter of some controversy. Some scholars see the incomplete lines of the Captain simply as an indication that his speech was cut down in production. At times, however, short lines are used to such brilliant effect that I am persuaded that they do indicate pauses. The dialogue between Macbeth and Banquo at the top of 3.1 contains several short lines, usually before or after questions. If you put pauses there, it gives their scene an awkward rhythm that suggests they are now suspicious of each other, as confirmed in their soliloquies, before and after the scene.

In Shakespeare, some short verse lines can be put together to create a complete blank verse line. Shakespeare gives Romeo and Juliet a shared verse line to emphasize their connection at the end of their sonnet when they first meet:

ROMEO
Give me my sin [kiss] again.
He kisses her [for the second time]
JULIET You kiss by th' book.[5]

There is another significant shared line at the end of that play:

CAPULET
O brother Montague, give me thy hand.
This is my daughter's jointure for no more
Can I demand.
MONTAGUE But I can give thee more
For I will ray [array] her statue in pure gold . . .[6]

Shakespeare uses this shared line to emphasize that Montague and Capulet, for the first time in the play, agree.

The Macbeths have many shared lines, which reinforce their intimacy, but we must be careful with such deductions. Shakespeare uses more shared lines in his later plays, where his verse is, in general, freer. Shared verse lines are set flush left in quartos and folios, but modern editions rearrange them, so that we can see how they form a complete verse line. In this staccato passage from *Macbeth*, the shared verse line accelerates the momentum and creates tension just after the murder of Duncan:

LADY MACBETH
Did you not speak?
MACBETH When?
LADY MACBETH Now.
MACBETH As I descended?[7]

Finally, it is important to remember that in scanning lines, *stress is relative to the foot it is in*. This frequently trips up those who are new to scansion. All accented syllables do not receive the same stress, and an unaccented syllable in one foot may receive more stress than the previous accented syllable in another. If this were not true blank verse would devolve into the dull heartbeat pattern in which it is often described: de-DUM de-DUM de-DUM de-DUM de-DUM.

Other verse variants

The use of four feet to a line, called tetrameter, gives a sing-song quality to lines, particularly if they are rhymed, and so it is often used for songs, poems, and the formality of the court entertainments known as masques. Shakespeare inserted masques into some of his later plays such as *The Tempest*, where the young lovers watch Prospero's playlet at the end of Act Four. Much (but not all) of the speech of *Macbeth*'s Weïrd Sisters is set apart by the use of seven-syllable lines of trochaic tetrameter that are missing the last unstressed syllable at the end:

/ – / – / – /
When shall |we three |meet a |gain?[8]

Another variant, rhyme, was used to accentuate. It adds lyricism to songs and prophesies. It underlines fervor in agitation or passion. It helps gild proverbs and maxims, as well as sententious thoughts. Rhyme helps to push the mediocre verse of Capulet's Wife over the top in the speech cited earlier; it underlines Orlando's bad poetry in *As You Like It* as well. Rhymed couplets had a formal function in Shakespeare's time. By convention, they were used to help us hear an aside, or to punctuate an exit or end of a speech or scene, a frequent use in *Romeo and Juliet*. Shakespeare gradually abandoned the use of rhyme of any kind. He peaked with rhyme in *Love's Labor's Lost*, where more than half of the lines are written in rhyme; *The Winter's Tale*, written near the end of his career, contains no rhymed lines in its dialogue.[9]

Shakespeare uses short lines, shared lines, trochees, and feminine endings more frequently in later plays such as *Macbeth*. The great Shakespearean director Michael Langham commented on this: "Always think of his plays, chronologically. (Shakespeare) seems always to be exploring, developing as his writing becomes more sophisticated. . . . No sooner has he set up his rules than he seems to break them."[10] One of the rules he broke was the use of prose.

Prose

Shakespeare began by writing to form, verse form, that was, to borrow Juliet's description of Romeo's kiss, "by th'book."[11] His early plays are largely in verse, with a limited use of prose, usually for working-class characters. As young playwrights often do, he followed models, in his case newly discovered ancient Roman plays, as well as contemporary English plays. The tragedies of Seneca influenced *Titus Andronicus*, and Marlowe's *Tamburlaine, Parts I and II* probably inspired the writing of the three parts of the history plays, *1–3 Henry VI*.

The bloom of high-flown poetry in the later plays of this period – *Love's Labour's Lost, Romeo and Juliet,* and *Richard II* – was a culmination for Shakespeare in his early experiments with verse. In the plays that immediately followed, some of his best and best known, he experimented with a high percentage of prose.

There is a limited use of prose in his history plays prior to *1–2 Henry IV*, his masterpieces in that form, but half of these two plays are in prose. An average of two-thirds of his great comedies, *As You Like It, Much Ado About Nothing*, and *Twelfth Night*, are written in prose.[12] In *As You Like It*, Rosalind, one of the smartest people in the Shakespeare canon and the daughter of a duke, is a prose speaker. The shepherd, Silvius, and his country lass, Phoebe, however, speak in verse because Shakespeare is parodying the conventions of pastoral poetry, a verse form. This should be a caution to those who would simply divide prose from verse speakers by class, particularly in this period.

Neil Bartlett summarizes Shakespeare's use of verse and prose in one play written in this period – *Twelfth Night*. In his program notes for the production he directed at the Goodman Theatre in Chicago, he wrote:

> People speak in poetry when they are being "elevated" or are in elevated situations. Olivia and Orsino, by virtue of their wealth and nobility, speak in verse all the time and even their language gets more poetical when the emotional or social temperature rises. Viola (a prose speaker) speaks in verse when the scene is very dramatic, as in the opening scene that follows the shipwreck, when she is trying to express her deepest feelings about the loss of her brother. Antonio speaks in verse because he is so in love . . . the verse gives the story great energy even when the actual characters themselves aren't elevated, but when the theatrical energy is.
>
> People speak in prose when they feel "real" – when they speak in the same basic language as the audience. The prose in [*Twelfth Night*] is particularly "real" – fresh, vivid, full of slang and colloquialisms . . . [but] we have to be very alert as to how people play with words, even when they are apparently just talking – how Sir Andrew tries to be clever, how Malvolio tries to be commanding and "posh," how Feste makes a living out of being clever.[13]

Writing so much prose seems to have liberated Shakespeare's writing, for the great tragedies that followed were written primarily in verse, but in a new, mature style. There is ease in his mastery of the verse that appears in them, and they are the summits of his verse writing. Prose is used when there is a lack of ease in the language of a character who would otherwise speak verse. Henry V and his future queen, Catherine of France, speak in prose to each other to emphasize their language barrier. Prose is used for other disjointed speech as well: for intoxication in *Antony and Cleopatra*, for frenzy in *Othello*, and for madness in *Lear*.[14] By convention prose was also used for written documents, proclamations, and letters, such as the one Lady Macbeth reads at her first entrance. Prose is also used as expected for low comedy, as with the Porter in *Macbeth*, but there is another good reason for him to speak in what Bartlett calls "the same basic language as the audience." As we will see in the chapter that focuses on him, the Porter has something important to ask us.

As we continue to investigate Shakespeare's use of verse, we must not get so caught up by "rules" that we miss the fine distinctions that Shakespeare is constantly making through language. Shakespeare differentiates verse speakers from one another: Romeo is not Juliet. Shakespeare does not always separate highborn from low by verse and prose, as already pointed out with Rosalind. He does not separate the world into lovers and clowns: Bottom, a working-class prose speaker, has the most eloquent speech in *A Midsummer Night's Dream*.

Shakespeare began and ended his career by writing primarily in verse. He perfected the blank verse line and then went on to extend sentences beyond the end of the verse line. *Macbeth* has many sentences that end in the middle of a line. This gives that verse variety. Shakespeare also began to use more trochees, feminine endings, short lines, and long lines as he proceeded in his career. By the era of the romances his blank verse is often so free that he does not seem to be using it.

We must listen carefully to how Shakespeare uses all the tools of language to create and differentiate his characters. In the next chapter, we will examine Shakespeare's use of another writer's tool, one that we are less familiar with today, and demonstrate how it quickly leads us to the heart of the most elusive speech in the play.

Notes

1 *Romeo and Juliet*, ed. Jill L. Levenson (Oxford World's Classics, 2000), 3.2.1–22.
2 Some contemporary editions add an apostrophe when the "e" is "dropp'd" to indicate that the -ed is not sounded, even though the full word is spelled out in the original editions.
3 Des McAnuff's production at La Jolla Playhouse in 1983.
4 David Mamet, *American Buffalo* (Grove Press, 1976), p. xi.
5 *Romeo and Juliet*, ed. Levenson, 1.4.223.
6 Ibid., 5.3.296–99.
7 *Macbeth*, ed. Nicholas Brooke (Oxford World Classics, 1994), 2.2.17.
8 Ibid., 1.1.1.
9 David Laurance Chambers, *The Metre of Macbeth* (Princeton, 1903), p. 68.
10 Michael Langham, "The Lightness of Shakespeare," *Journal for Stage Directors & Choreographers* 14, no. 1 (Spring/Summer 2000), p. 13. Langham

followed Tyrone Guthrie as the second Artistic Director of the Stratford Festival of Canada and the Guthrie Theatre in Minneapolis.

11 *Romeo and Juliet*, ed. Jill L. Levenson (Oxford World's Classics, 2000), 1.4.223.
12 David Laurance Chambers, *The Metre of Macbeth*, p. 68.
13 Neil Bartlett, Goodman Theatre Playbill, *Twelfth Night*, 1992.
14 E. A. Abbott, *A Shakespearean Grammar* (Dover, 1966), p. 429.

Bibliography

Shakespeare editions cited

Macbeth. Ed. Nicholas Brooke. Oxford World Classics, 1994.
Romeo and Juliet. Ed. Jill L. Levenson. Oxford World's Classics, 2000.

Other sources

Abbott, E. A. *A Shakespearean Grammar*. Dover, 1966.
Bartlett, Neil. Goodman Theatre Playbill, *Twelfth Night*, 1992.
Chambers, David Laurance. *The Metre of Macbeth*. Princeton University, 1903.
Langham, Michael. "The Lightness of Shakespeare." *The Journal for Stage Directors & Choreographers* 14, no. 1 (Spring/Summer 2000).
Mamet, David. *American Buffalo*. Grove Press, 1976.

5 Mercutio's use of rhetoric

The name, Marcuccio, appears in one of the series of novellas that are the source material for *Romeo and Juliet*, where he is one of Rosaline's suitors and not involved in Tybalt's death. The character of Mercutio, however, is Shakespeare's creation, which should alert us to pay attention to what his presence adds to the play.

Like Falstaff, Mercutio is full of life, and his exuberance is one of the reasons we are so fascinated by him. He is moody, however, even beyond what we may expect from a young man. He talks about this in 3.1, where he accuses the mild-mannered Benvolio of being hot-tempered, when he is clearly describing himself. Benvolio's opening lines are in verse, but Shakespeare then switches to prose to emphasize Mercutio's disjointed mood:

> Thou art as hot a jack [knave] in thy mood as any in Italy; and as soon moved to be moody, and as soon moody to be moved [to strike].[1]

Mercutio is a master of rhetoric, and here he uses rhetorical repetitions to emphasize the key words. It is not necessary to remember their formidable names, but it is important to understand how they function in an aural medium. In the quote above, the repetition of a word or phrase at the beginning of a sentence, clause or phrase is called *anaphora* (uh-NAF-or-uh). Here, the repetition of "as soon" helps us follow the sense of the line by alerting us to listen carefully to the inversion of words that follow. Inverting the order of "moved" and "moody" – *antimetabole* (an-tye-muh-TAB-uh-lee) – makes the point and in a witty way: he is as quickly moved to be moody as, once moody, quickly moved to strike. The choice of the word "moved" is a deliberate echo of the opening of the play, where the phrase "quickly moved to strike" is tossed back and forth by Sampson and Gregory. Both scenes are constructed to remind us of the other. Sampson's bravado is false; we soon learn that Mercutio's is not.

To understand this scene, we need to examine what has gone before. A stage direction announces Mercutio's first entrance in 1.4: "Enter Romeo, Mercutio, Benvolio with five or six other masquers [and] torch-bearers."[2] They are on their way to Juliet's debut at Capulet's masquerade ball. Only the three named characters speak. Why does Shakespeare include the others? The reactions of an onstage audience can help us to understand Romeo and Mercutio's complicated verbal joust. It also reveals something about Mercutio's character: he likes having an audience. Later, this will work against him when Tybalt embarrasses him in front of their entourages before their duel.

Returning to 1.4, the use of torches in an outdoor theatre where performances took place in the afternoon indicates that it is now evening in Verona. Note how Shakespeare uses that prop to beget the train of imagery that follows. I have italicized the repetition of words (*ploce*, PLAW-see) and words derived from the same root (*polytptoton*, puh-LIP-tuh-tan), such as love/lover. Note that Mercutio continually inverts and twists Romeo's words (*antimetabole*, underlined below) both to mock him and to lead the imagery, step by step, to the conclusion:

ROMEO
Give me a torch, I am not for this ambling;
Being but *heavy* I will bear [carry] the light . . .
MERCUTIO
You are a *lover*; borrow Cupid's wings,
And soar with them above a common bound [leap] . . .
ROMEO
Under <u>*love's heavy burden do I sink*</u>.
MERCUTIO
And, to <u>*sink* in it, should you *burden love*,</u>
Too great oppression for a *tender thing*.
ROMEO
Is *love* a *tender thing*? It is *too rough*,
Too rude, *too* boist'rous, and it *pricks* like thorn.
MERCUTIO
If <u>*love be rough with you, be rough with love;*</u>
Prick love for *pricking* and you beat it down.[3]

Romeo riffs off a word for the torch – "light" – and repeats the word "heavy" to dramatize his mood. A variant of the word "love" occurs seven times because love is the subject of the dialogue. Mercutio introduces sexual allusions into the dialogue and blurs the distinction between love and lust by inverting the word order twice. In the last line, he gives his solution for a horny young man – masturbation.

Polyptoton also binds together the lines that follow, where repetition from the same root enhances the wit in their attempt to best each other.[4] Romeo tells Mercutio that "he *dreamt* a *dream*" last night; Mercutio gets the better of him by suggesting "that *dreamers* often lie." Romeo protests that "they do *dream* things true." Mercutio now extends this theme to top Romeo with an extended improvisation on the fairy Mab, the midwife of dreams. It is full of deliciously described, but seemingly pointless detail and is an elusive speech to pin down. As with many fabricators, however, Mercutio reveals more than he realizes and certainly more than most productions take into account.

Mercutio's long speech can be best parsed by separating it into sections based on Shakespeare's use of *anaphora*: beginning clauses with the same word or words helps the audience hear the speech as a series of lists. It also helps the actor create the acceleration that gives the speech its build, as Mercutio spirals progressively out of control. The first section is a detailed description of Mab's chariot. The word "her" is repeated at the beginning of the items in the list. I have italicized the use of anaphora throughout the speech:[5]

> *Her* chariot is an empty hazelnut
> Made by the joiner squirrel or old grub,
> Time out o' mind the fairies' coachmakers.[6]
> *Her* wagon-spokes made of long spinners' legs;[7]
> The cover[8] of the wings of grasshoppers;
> *Her* traces[9] of the smallest spider web;
> *Her* collars of the moonshine's wat'ry beams;
> *Her* whip of cricket's bone, the lash of film;
> *Her* wagoner, a small grey-coated gnat,
> Not half so big as a round little worm
> Pricked from the lazy finger of a maid . . .

For the next section, Shakespeare changes the repeated word so we can hear this new list as a separate one, as we join Mab's nightly journey:

> And in this state she gallops night by night
> Through lovers' brains, and then they dream of love;
> *O'er*[10] courtiers' knees, that dream on curtsies straight;
> *O'er* lawyers' fingers who straight dream on fees;
> *O'er* ladies lips, who straight on kisses dream,
> Which oft the angry Mab with blisters plagues,
> Because their breaths with sweetmeats tainted are . . .

This list is shorter than the previous one, which gives an acceleration to the speech. Note that Mab brings welcome dreams to the dreamers, but the section ends in a darker image than that of the first list. "Sweetmeats" may also be taken as the male organ and blisters an indication of the sexual disease that results.

The wish list continues. Each of the next group of dreamers is introduced with the repetition of the word "sometime," which Shakespeare alternates with "(and) then." Note that the repetition of the word "of" accelerates at the end and contributes to the increasing frenzy of the speech:

> *Sometime* she gallops o'er a courtier's nose,
> *And then* dreams he *of* smelling out a suit;
> And *sometime* comes she with a tithe-pig's tail,
> Tickling a parson's nose as a [he] lies asleep –
> *Then* he dreams *of* another benefice.
> *Sometime* she driveth o'er a soldier's neck
> *And then* dreams he *of* cutting foreign throats,
> *Of* breaches, ambuscados, Spanish blades,
> *Of* healths five fathoms deep; *and then* anon
> Drums in his ear, at which he starts and wakes,
> And being thus frighted, swears a prayer or two
> And sleeps again.

Mab brings dark visions at the end of the above section, and an even darker one follows. The pace becomes wilder, as does the repeated use of the emphatics – "this" and "that."

> . . . *This* is *that* very Mab
> *That* plaits the manes of horses in the night,
> And bakes the elf-locks in foul, sluttish hairs,
> Which once untangled much misfortune bodes.
> *This* is the hag, when maids lie on their backs,
> *That* presses them and learns them first to bear,
> Making them women of good carriage.
> *This* is she –

Romeo interrupts his friend with these words: "Peace, peace, Mercutio, peace, / Thou talk'st of nothing." The repetition of a word, such as "peace", with no other word intervening, is called *epizeuxis* (eh-puh-ZOOK-sis). Its most famous use in Shakespeare is Lear's "Howl, howl, howl, howl, howl, howl, howl" upon entering with his dead daughter at the end of that play. It is reserved for extreme moments, as here, where

Romeo must repeat the word "peace" three times in order to stop Mercutio from continuing.

The use of *anaphora* in the Mab speech not only helps the audience *hear* its structure by breaking it into four sections, but also leads us to the heart of these elusive lines. The first two sections end with slurs on women:

> Not half so big as a round little worm
> Prick'd from the lazy finger of a maid . . .
>
> O'er ladies lips, who straight on kisses dream,
> Which oft the angry Mab with blisters plagues
> Because their breaths with sweetmeats tainted are . . .

Women are not the subject of the third list, but the fourth is a continuous assault on them. "Foul, sluttish hairs" are the pubic hairs which "once untangled" lead to misfortune, and Mercutio tells us what happens "when maids lie on their backs."

Mercutio follows Romeo's interdiction to stop talking with these words and returns to the subject of dreams that introduced this speech:

> . . . True, I talk of dreams,
> Which are the children of an idle brain,
> Begot of nothing but vain fantasy,
> Which is as thin of substance as the air,
> And more inconstant than the wind who woos
> Even now the frozen bosom of the north;
> And being angered, puffs away from thence,
> Turning his side to the dew-dropping south.[11]

This coded speech is accurate to the proceedings we have witnessed. Romeo is the inconstant wind who woos the frozen bosom of Rosaline. He gets angry and cries on the shoulders of his friends, who have to put up with both his ill-humor and his absence. Shakespeare observes a group dynamic that we can still understand today. Teenage boys hang in a pack; one of them falls in love. The dynamics of the pack are forever altered. Mercutio's anger in the Mab speech, however, seems to go even deeper than this, as it slips out in progressively harsher images towards women. His youth may temper our response to his words, but at the very least he seems insecure about women and perhaps even sex, despite his facade of sexual bravado.

Before we continue to follow the tangle of relationships presented here, I want to examine the fundamental importance of rhetoric to the spoken word and to theatre dialogue at this time.

Rhetoric

There were no grammar books in Shakespeare's day. There was an unofficial grammar, but it was not yet codified. Elizabethan students studied rhetoric in school instead. Today we construct units of thought according to principles of *grammar*. In Shakespeare's time, Elizabethans used rhetoric to help us hear the units of thought, instead of *grammar*. I just used a rhetorical figure called *epistrophe* (ep-ISS-struh-fee). Repeating the same word at the end of a line also emphasizes the key word. Later the development of grammar became essential to authors who wrote for a printed medium, but it is less useful in an aural medium such as theatre where organizing by sound sense is more helpful.

Brian Vickers in his excellent, concise introduction to rhetoric describes a number of rhetorical devices. For the purposes of my book, I will ignore those that we are more familiar with, tropes such as metaphor, and focus on figures – the repetitions of words and parallel structures that help us *hear* the structure of language. Repetition and parallel structures offer an aural way of creating comparisons, moving from one sphere of thought to another, which is the basis of poetic language. It is also a more active way of engaging the audience than metaphor, because in using metaphor playwrights make the connection for us. With figures of rhetoric we must make the connection ourselves. Any time we in the audience make the connection, the playwright is engaging our minds. This participation is key to understanding Shakespeare's art.

Vickers uses an analogy to musical notation to distinguish tropes and figures.[12] I find it helpful to use this context to define figures in this way: if words *provide* the melody of Shakespeare's language and verse *provides* the rhythm, figures *provide* the phrasing. As in music, phrasing offers another way of breaking up the steady drumbeat of the rhythm. It also provides more. In my previous sentence, the repetition of "provides" (*ploce*) and the parallel construction (*parison* – PA-ris-uhn) helps us hear the *structure* of the sentence. Because of this, the idea being expressed becomes clearer. Take out the repeated word "provide" in the first sentence of this paragraph and what we are hearing subliminally is:

Words . . . melody
Verse . . . rhythm
Rhetoric . . . phrasing

Verbal repetition is still a fundamental tool of playwriting. Mamet is celebrated for the rhythm he created in his use of repetition in *American Buffalo*. It helps create the musicality of his lines. His verbal play also helps keep us alert and engaged, connecting the thoughts in an aural medium.

Puns are another form of rhetoric. I have already pointed out two in Chapter 1. "Collier . . . choler . . . collar" is a series of homophonic puns or *paronomasia*, words that sound alike but have different meanings. The phrase "heartless hinds" uses semantic puns or *syllepsis*: each word has two meanings. *Antanaclasis* is another kind of pun in which words are repeated with a different meaning, such as the one at the end of this section.

Rhetoric was originally developed by the Greeks for speaking in courts of law and in arguing in government. For this reason there are rhetorical figures that promote the construction of an argument, as when the repeated word ends one clause or sentence and begins another, so that we can follow the progression of the argument being made. The term for this is *anadiplosis* (an-uh-duh-PLOH-sus).

Rhetoric must be connected with sense or it devolves to its pejorative connotation and sounds "rhetorical." Shakespeare is capable of using this to characterize someone. Just as Capulet's Wife mangles poetry in her speech in 1.3, Polonius overuses rhetoric. Gertrude admonishes him for this when she tells him to use "More matter with less art."[13] Romeo would have been schooled in rhetoric, and he also uses it precociously. As with his poetry, he is a bit self-conscious and flashy in its use. Shakespeare uses this to help us understand who Romeo is at the beginning of the play.

Vickers makes this observation about the evolution of rhetoric in Shakespeare's plays: "Shakespeare developed from stiffness to flexibility . . . he absorbs [rhetoric] into the tissue of living dramatic speech until he re-creates thought and feeling with a freshness that conceals his art."[14] Vickers cites the line when Othello extinguishes a candle, as he is about to kill Desdemona: "Put out the light, and then put out the light!"[15] Never has there been a more eloquent and heartrending use of a pun in the English language.

The turning point

Returning to the scene at the top of Act Three, Tybalt enters and says (italics added):

TYBALT Gentlemen, good e'en, a word with one of *you*.
MERCUTIO And but one word with one of us? Couple it with something; make it a word and a blow.
TYBALT *You* shall find me apt enough to that, sir, an [if] *you* will give me occasion.
MERCUTIO Could *you* not take some occasion without giving?
TYBALT Mercutio, *thou* consortest with Romeo.
MERCUTIO "Consort"! What dost *thou* make us minstrels? An *thou* make minstrels of us, look to hear nothing but discords. Here's my fiddlestick; here's that shall make you dance. *Zounds*, "consort"![16]

Many languages still use two words for *you* singular today, as was customary in Shakespeare's time. Tybalt uses *you* plural in his first line to address two people: Benvolio is also present. Tybalt and Mercutio then address each other with the formal *you* singular, as they are acquaintances but certainly not friends. *Thou* was used to indicate a friendly familiarity or to impose familiarity on someone in a lower position, such as a servant or wife. After Mercutio pushes Tybalt to a confrontation, Tybalt changes to *thou*, a deliberate insult if the proper address should have been *you*, as it relegated that person to a lower rank. It indicates that the emotional temperature of the scene has risen and that "Thou *consortest* with Romeo" is a serious insult, not a reprimand for being Romeo's friend. That Mercutio understands it as an insult is indicated by his own use of *thou* twice in his reply.

Mercutio now draws his "fiddlestick" (his sword) and uses a swear word that tells us just how angry he is. Earlier in the play, both Gregory and the Nurse use the oath *marry*. Even Capulet's Wife uses it when she is annoyed. Short for "by the Virgin Mary," it was considered a mild oath because it doesn't use God's name. *Zounds,* meaning "by God's wounds," does. Its rarity in Shakespeare tells us that Tybalt has struck a nerve.

The nerve that is struck can be found in the *OED*. *Consort* as a noun means "companion" or "spouse." The verb *consort* means "to keep company with," but the *OED* goes on to add an obsolete meaning: "to have sexual commerce with." The *OED* lists the first recorded use of *consort* with that meaning in 1600,[17] but the new Arden edition of *Romeo and Juliet* states that "Mercutio's stung response suggests the meaning may have been around earlier."[18] Tybalt has just called Mercutio a fag in public. Even if Tybalt only meant to say, Mercutio, you are a friend of Romeo, that is not the way Mercutio takes it. He goes ballistic, and the double meanings of his reply suggest how he understands the charge: "I will budge for no man's pleasure, I." The rhetorical repetition of "I" at the beginning and end of that sentence is called *epanalepsis* (ehp-un-nuh-LEP-sis) and is used to make the line pop.

Until recently, writers on this play have overlooked or chosen to overlook the simple, obvious situation here, perhaps because Shakespeare dares to bring in one of Elizabethan society's taboos. When I worked on my first production of *Romeo and Juliet* at La Jolla Playhouse in 1983, a discussion of this aspect of the play rarely made it into print, certainly not into editions that could be sold in secondary schools. By the time McAnuff directed his second production in Stratford, Canada, in 2008, that taboo had been lifted.

Because Mercutio looks obsessively for Romeo following Capulet's party, it is now sometimes argued that he is in love with Romeo. I believe Shakespeare leaves that question open. Perhaps he had to be ambiguous because of Elizabethan laws against homosexuality. Perhaps he leaves the answer to that question to us because he seems to be more interested in the results of our actions than in their motivations. This is an important aspect of Shakespeare's writing that I will continue to explore in this book. How does the *accusation* of homosexuality add to our understanding of the play? The film director George Stevens told Shelley Winters during the filming of *A Place in the Sun* that her job as an actor was to discover how her role contributed to the whole.[19] How does the character of Mercutio contribute to the whole?

In the opening scene of the play, Tybalt taunted the Montagues by calling them a bunch of women.[20] His taunt to Mercutio is an extension of that accusation. After Mercutio is killed, Romeo draws his sword to fight Tybalt with these words: "O sweet Juliet, / Thy beauty hath made me effeminate."[21] What's in a word? Words can be as deadly as weapons in this play. The words "consort" and "effeminate" defeat two of the most vital characters in it. That is why it is important to understand both the nature of Tybalt's accusation and Mercutio's susceptibility to it, whether true or not. In *Romeo and Juliet*, Shakespeare examines love in its many manifestations. Sexual tensions and insecurities are a repeated source of violence in the play. Mercutio is the first to die in this pattern. That is how he contributes to our understanding of the play.

Romeo and Juliet flirts with forms in many ways that are modern. It is both a comedy and a tragedy. It is both an Aristotelian tragedy of character, in Romeo's actions, and a Senecan tragedy of fate, in its unstoppable cycle of violence. The lovers are pulled into that violence by outside events, but also bear some responsibility. There is yet another aspect of the public story to be examined that will lead us to a second source of violence.

Notes

1 *Romeo and Juliet*, ed. Jill L. Levenson (Oxford World's Classics, 2000), 3.1.11–13.
2 Ibid., 1.4.0 (stage direction).
3 Ibid., 1.4.9–26.
4 Ibid., 1.4.48–50.
5 Ibid., 1.4.57–94.
6 The excellent Oxford World's Classics edition that I have been citing follows the authoritative Q2's placement of the first three lines quoted here *after* "from the lazy finger of a maid." Most editions treat this as a printing error and reposition them to the top of this sequence, where I have placed them, so that the image of the chariot is set up before the detail of its components.
7 "Spinners" are the spider-like insect known as daddy-long-legs.
8 The protective cover over the wheels.
9 "Traces" connect the chariot to the harness ("collar") of the animal pulling it.
10 As many editions do, I have substituted Q1's use of "O'er" here; the good Oxford editor, Jill Levenson, follows the authoritative Q2 in using "On."
11 Ibid., Levenson, 1.4.94–101.

12 Brian Vickers, "Shakespeare's Use of Rhetoric," in *A New Companion to Shakespeare Studies*, eds. Kenneth Muir and S. Schoenbaum (Cambridge University, 1971), p. 87.
13 *Hamlet*, ed. Harold Jenkins, Arden Second Series (Methuen, 1982), 2.2.95.
14 Vickers, "Shakespeare's Use of Rhetoric," p. 91.
15 *Othello*, ed. E. A. J. Honigmann, Arden Second Series (Thomas Nelson & Sons, 1999), 5.2.7.
16 *Romeo and Juliet*, ed. Levenson, 3.1.37–48. E'en for even' or evening could indicate any time after noon. Mercutio says, "The day is hot," at 3.1.2.
17 *Oxford English Dictionary* (Oxford University Press, 1971), sb. con'/sort, 1 and 3; v. con/sort', 1, 2, and 5c.
18 *Romeo and Juliet*, ed. René Weis, Arden Third Series (Bloomsbury, 2012), see footnote on 3.1.44.
19 From *Inside the Actor's Studio*: A television interview with Shelley Winters, November 13, 1994.
20 Tybalt called them "heartless hinds." *Romeo and Juliet*, ed. Levenson, note 9 on 1.1.62–63.
21 Ibid., Levenson, 3.1.113–14.

Bibliography

Shakespeare editions cited

Hamlet. Ed. Harold Jenkins, Arden Second Series. Methuen, 1982.
Othello. Ed. E.A.J. Honigmann. Thomas Nelson & Sons, 1999.
Romeo and Juliet. Ed. Jill L. Levenson. Oxford World's Classics, 2000.
Romeo and Juliet. Ed. René Weis, Arden Third Series. Bloomsbury, 2012.

Other sources

Lipton, James. Television interview with Shelley Winters. *Inside the Actor's Studio*. November 13, 1994.
Oxford English Dictionary. Oxford University Press, 1971.
Vickers, Brian. "Shakespeare's Use of Rhetoric." In *A New Companion to Shakespeare Studies*, eds. Kenneth Muir and S. Schoenbaum. Cambridge, 1971, pp. 83–88.

6 Three households

The Prologue promised us a second, public story: "The continuance of their parents rage." The Montagues and the Capulets may be both "alike in dignity," but Shakespeare creates individuals here as elsewhere, not generic parents who are interchangeable. They produce very different children, for one, and in trying to understand the families it is fair to take the characteristics of their progeny into account. Other clues are there right from the beginning.

The Capulets

Shakespeare provides a considerable amount of stage time for the Capulets, often in scenes that are cut down in production because of a failure to understand who they are, and how that contributes to the play.

Capulet is one of the largest roles and one of the play's most compelling characters. If you believe Capulet is enticing Paris to court Juliet in his first scene with him, then he is smart and shrewd, a man who understands how to size up and manipulate people. In their first scene, he invites Paris to view her at his "poor" house, which it is certainly not.[1] That Capulet can afford a large ball attests to considerable wealth. In fact, words connected with money pepper the scene. He uses an unusual word, "inherit," for all the beauties Paris will see at the feast and tells him that Juliet, in "reck'ning," is second to none.[2] Later at the ball, the Nurse reminds us of that wealth when she tells Romeo that "he that can lay hold of her [Juliet] / Shall have the chinks."[3] Money also invades the vocabulary of the progeny of both the Capulets and the Montagues. Romeo famously refers to Juliet as "merchandise" in the balcony scene,[4] and Juliet expresses her happiness with their marriage in this way: "They are but beggars that can count their worth; / But my true love is grown to such excess, / I cannot sum up sum of half my wealth."[5]

Capulet is a man of seeming contradictions. His first lines at the feast, where he may be inebriated, suggest that he is not well educated:

> Welcome, gentlemen. Ladies that have their toes
> Unplagued with corns will walk a bout [dance a turn] with you.
> Ah my mistresses, which of you all
> Will now deny to dance? She that makes dainty,
> She I'll swear hath corns . . . And foot it girls![6]

Later, however, when he believes Juliet to be dead, he speaks some of the most eloquent poetry in the play: "Death lies on her like an untimely frost / Upon the sweetest flower of all the field."[7]

Capulet is unexpectedly gracious in allowing Romeo to stay at the ball even after he discovers who he is, but he does not tolerate disobedience within his household. He is furious that Tybalt will not listen to him at the feast, and later focuses his considerable wrath on Juliet when she refuses to marry Paris. When he talks about Juliet in his scenes with Paris, however, it is clear that he loves her. As for Juliet, she seems to be her father's child, smart and willful like him. Once either has made a decision – Juliet to marry Romeo, Capulet that she marry Paris – they cannot be moved.

As mentioned before, the Lord and Lady designations of the Capulets and the Montagues are not in the source texts and are particularly misleading when we try to understand the Capulets. Capulet has the roughness of a driven self-made man who has moved up in the world. If we recognize Capulet as new money, many of the contradictions that mark his character will fall into place.

Biographical speculation must always be treated as suspect and so should mine, but in *Will in the World*, Stephen Greenblatt draws a portrait of Shakespeare's upwardly mobile father that, apart from the level of wealth, seems very like Capulet to me.[8] John Shakespeare came from a family of farmers, became a successful merchant of leather goods, and eventually, High Bailiff, the rough equivalent of mayor of Stratford. This is not just idle speculation: Romeo's comments about money later in the play have an edge that seems personal. Perhaps one of the reasons Shakespeare spends so much time with the Capulets is because he understood that family. As did another *arriviste*, Gatsby, Capulet throws parties to improve his social standing. When he is drunk, however, his background peeps through.

The marriage to Paris is a key to understanding this family. There are actually three households in the play: Paris and Mercutio are kinsmen to the Prince. Marriage to a kinsman to the Prince is a big deal for this upwardly mobile family. After a Capulet kills Mercutio, the marriage becomes a political necessity.

The Montagues

If this sounds like conjecture, compare the Capulets to the Montagues. The latter have only a few scenes, but the differences with the Capulets are striking. When they first enter, Capulet's Wife criticizes her husband in public; Montague's Wife expresses concern for hers: "Thou shalt not stir one foot to seek a foe."[9]

Capulet is largely defined through his relationship with their daughter. After their first brief exchange, Capulet and his wife do not speak to each other onstage until they unite in their attack on Juliet, two-thirds of the way through the play, for refusing to marry Paris. The Montagues, by contrast, are presented as a unit right at the top of the play in their only long scene together. Both husband and his wife express concern about their absent son: "Could we but learn from whence his sorrows grow, / We would as willingly give cure as know."[10] At the end of the play, Montague genuinely mourns the death of his wife with these words: "Grief of my son's exile hath stopped her breath."[11]

The Montagues seem to be a more stable family than the Capulets, and there is a certain formality and gravity to their language. This family uses classical allusions. Montague refers to Aurora; his son to Dian's wit, Titan's wheels, Cynthia's brows. We do not find these in the language of Mr. and Mrs. Capulet, although Juliet does refer to Apollo and Phaëton in her "Gallop apace" speech. If Romeo is an indication of who the Montagues are, they are well educated. Romeo has the language of a well-read young man and the self-centered ease of the scion of a family that is comfortable with their money, and perhaps a bit indolent because of it. The Montagues behave like old landed money.

Historical and societal context in *Romeo and Juliet* that would have been unmistakable to Shakespeare's audiences may be elusive for us today. Shakespeare was writing at a time when England was moving from a feudal system with land-based wealth into an early modern society based on merchandise. That is why merchants take center stage in plays of this period, such as *Comedy of Errors* and *The Merchant of Venice*. Merry Old England (if it ever existed as such) was quickly becoming the past. *Twelfth Night* is another record of this, and a useful analog to understanding the acrimony between classes that fuels *Romeo and Juliet*. In *Twelfth Night*, indolent knights like Sir Toby were becoming obsolete, while coolly efficient Puritans like Malvolio were moving into positions of power. The class hatred between Toby and Malvolio is there from the beginning and continues to the last lines of the play. Indeed, forty years later the Puritans would take over the government, close the theatres and execute the King.

In *Romeo and Juliet*, Shakespeare is writing about the new merchant class in Elizabethan England and the tensions that it created with the old landed gentry. "The *continuance* of their parents' rage" shows old and new money jockeying for standing. That is why rank and status is such a prevalent motif in the play from its first lines. That is why the Capulets are so excited about Juliet's debut at the ball and her wedding to Paris. He is a "golden story," in the words of Capulet's Wife, for this upwardly mobile family; as cousin to the Prince, he is a good catch. Class tensions and hatred were particularly strong at this time because of the extreme shift in the social order, as England began to move into the early modern age. Class tensions remain relevant to our world today and so it is important to acknowledge them in mounting this play. In the next sections, we will continue to explore the issues of class and status in *Romeo and Juliet* as it is articulated in a series of what I call "odd scenes."

Odd scenes

Odd scenes are often cut down or cut out because their purpose is elusive. It is usually necessary to identify some cuts before rehearsals begin because rehearsal time is seldom ideal, but with Shakespeare it is a mistake to cut an entire scene before an attempt is made to discover, while seeing on its feet, why Shakespeare has included it, particularly in the later plays, as he mastered the art of playwriting in the course of his career. In addition, scenes or sections of scenes we may eventually decide to cut can provide clues to what issues were circling in his head.

There is a good example in *1 Henry IV*. Prince Hal and Poins are waiting for Falstaff to arrive at the tavern. They play a prank on a young waiter, Francis, making him rush back and forth between two rooms by constantly calling for him in both. The scene goes on for three pages and usually understood as comic relief. That is often the fallback position that scholars use to describe scenes they do not understand. For a long time the Porter scene in *Macbeth* was described only in this way. Weeks into *Henry* rehearsals, we decided to give this section a final shot before cutting it.[12] Hal asks the indentured waiter this:

PRINCE How long hast thou to serve, Francis?
FRANCIS Forsooth, five years . . .
PRINCE A long lease for the clinking of pewter; but Francis, darest thou be so valiant as to play the coward with thy indenture, and show it a pair of heels, and run away from it?[13]

In the course of playing the scene, John Vickery, the actor playing Hal, suddenly understood the connection between the Prince and the servant. What began as a joke leads Hal to contemplate his own indenture, his service as Prince to his country, something that he has shirked. That is why Hal abruptly switches the subject and mocks his rival, Hotspur, the model son who has not walked away from his duties: "I am not yet of Percy's mind, the Hotspur of the north, he that kills me some six or seven dozens of Scots at a breakfast, washes his hands, and says to his wife, 'Fie upon this quiet life, I want some work'."[14] An intuitive leap made by an actor on his feet led us to penetrate this elusive and important sequence in the play. The actor was so in the moment that he realized why he was saying the words in this sequence as he was saying them, and so we in the rehearsal room did as well.

This kind of discovery is something actors try to recreate during performance. In contemporary theatre, actors often pause to think and then say the line. That only slows down verse and makes it harder to understand the sense. McAnuff learned from Michael Langham, one of his predecessors as Artistic Director of the Stratford Shakespeare Festival, that getting the thought on the line, as you speak the word, makes the verse live. Langham called this "living thought." It became central to Des's work with actors on Shakespeare's plays, and it works.

The public story of *Romeo and Juliet* is brought to a conclusion with a series of odd scenes that demonstrate some of the issues that arise when deciding if an elusive scene should be cut, cut down, or kept intact. At the end of Act Four, the Capulets, the Nurse, and Paris mourn loudly over the body of what they think is the dead Juliet. The Nurse's lamentations are heartfelt and clearly intended to be comic, but after an eloquent pair of lines from Capulet what are we to make of the over-the-top wailing from him, his wife, and Paris? They seem to try to outdo each other, and their words betray that their primary concern is *their* loss. Note that Capulet's Wife implies that she does not "rejoice and solace" in her relationship with her husband (italics added):

CAPULET

Death is my son-in-law, Death is my heir . . .

CAPULET'S WIFE

But *one* thing to rejoice and solace in,
And cruel Death hath catched it from my sight . . .

PARIS

Beguiled, divorcèd, wrongèd, spited, slain![15]

This scene is difficult to bring off emotionally because of the boldness of Shakespeare's conception in returning to a comedic tone at this point in the play. Perhaps we lacked the courage to allow the wailing to be as outrageous as the lines suggest, but I think that the scene is overwritten. Shakespeare's ability at this stage in his career does not yet match his conception, and we must acknowledge when this happens, even in Shakespeare. I have never seen the lamentation scene work without its lines cut down and its humor cut back. Shakespeare does provide a nonverbal tool to guide us through this section. Friar Laurence knows the truth, and his silent reaction to their words can indicate how we should feel about these lamentations. Eventually, the Friar will nail the Capulets with the line: "The most you sought was her *promotion* [italics added],"[16] a choice of a word that brings rank and class back into the play. Shakespeare leaves us with some sympathy for the Capulets at the end of the play, but I believe their final scene is more moving, if we acknowledge their selfishness here by retaining some of the lamentations.

Our fight director for the La Jolla production worked on twenty-eight productions of *Romeo and Juliet* and had never seen the next scene. At the end of Act Four, Paris brings three musicians to greet his bride on their wedding day, and they remain onstage with the Nurse after the rest have left. The Nurse dismisses the musicians with the words, "This is a pitiful case." The First Musician replies, "The case may be amended."[17] From his point of view the pitiful case is theirs: they have lost their gig and he is asking to be paid. The Nurse exits and sends in her servant Peter. The stage direction in Q2 says, "Enter Will Kemp,"[18] the company's leading clown at the time, so we know we are in for a comic diversion.

Peter asks the musicians to play the song, "Heart's Ease." The First Musician declines and they get into a verbal fight that quickly escalates. It is a comedic take on the fights in 1.1 and 3.1, and as in those scenes they insult each other's rank:

FIRST MUSICIAN What will you give us?
PETER No money, on my faith, but the gleek [an obscene gesture]. I will give you the minstrel.
FIRST MUSICIAN Then I will give you the serving-creature.
PETER Then I will lay the serving-creature's dagger on your pate . . .
SECOND MUSICIAN Pray you, put up your dagger and put out your wit.[19]

Peter then asks them a question about the song's lyrics (italics added): "Why 'music with her *silver* sound'?" He rejects their answers and provides his own: "because musicians have no gold for sounding."[20] The musicians are not worth gold coins – and he leaves without paying them. To make this clear McAnuff had Peter enter with a prop that is implied in the text, a purse of coins, and had Peter shake it in their faces. What can a poor boy do? The musicians decide to "tarry for the mourners, and stay dinner"[21] to get free food at the wake.

It is particularly tempting to cut this scene in its entirety because in contemporary theatre we are used to a play accelerating here, just where Elizabethan dramas frequently seem to dawdle. Shakespeare, however, often slips in some his most eloquent realizations at the end of Act Four. Think of Bottom's dream, or Rosalind's "I should have been a woman by right,"[22] or Prospero's "We are such stuff / As dreams are made on, and our little life / Is rounded with a sleep."[23] The eloquent realization in *Romeo and Juliet* doesn't appear until the scene that follows, but retaining the key lines in the musicians' scene helps to set it up.

What's in a word?

The musicians' scene is usually cut in its entirety; the apothecary scene is usually cut down. Romeo is seeking poison so that he can join Juliet in death. The scene begins with his description of the apothecary shop, which sets up the location, but why does he go on at such length? A family of words pepper his speech: tattered, meager, misery, worn to the bones, beggarly, penury, poor, caitiff, needy.[24] The actor playing Romeo must say at least some of them because they are part of a chain of thoughts that leads to a realization.

The Apothecary cannot sell mortal drugs in Mantua under pain of death, and so Romeo persuades him to break the law: "Famine is in thy cheeks, / Need and oppression starveth in thine eyes . . . The world affords no law to make thee rich."[25] Money now makes its most forceful appearance in the play. The musicians asked for silver; Romeo pays the Apothecary with gold:

> There is thy gold [coins], worse poison to men's souls,
> Doing more murder in this loathsome world,
> Than these poor compounds that thou mayst not sell.
> I sell thee poison; thou hast sold me none.
> Farewell, buy food, and get thyself in flesh.[26]

Capulet's Wife refers to Paris as a "golden story" in Act One. Shakespeare reintroduces "gold" in the musicians' scene because he often explores his ideas across the full spectrum of society. In the apothecary scene, a new, more reflective Romeo calls gold "poison" *twice* because he now associates the wealth that makes the families so powerful with the violence that the Prince cannot contain. Juliet becomes a commodity in her parents' pursuit of it. Romeo becomes part of the cycle of violence that sustains it. Does the death of their children end the violence, as the Prologue promised?

The last scene of the play has the same structure as its parallel scenes at the top and in the middle of the play. Two men quarrel and swords are drawn. Paris and Romeo die, Juliet dies, and the death of Montague's Wife is announced. We have discussed the importance of Paris's death and the suicides of the two lovers. I want to focus on the long sequence that follows. The Capulets, the Montagues, and the Prince now enter, as they do in 1.1 and 3.1. The post-fight sections of those scenes last about two pages each. The equivalent section of this final scene is five pages and is extensively cut down in most productions. We already know the information that the Friar and the Pages tell the assembled community. Why does Shakespeare recount it again and at such length? The answer is to be found not in the words of the script, but in the implied staging.

In McAnuff's production, the speakers faced upstage; the three households faced the audience. This allowed the audience to focus on the non-verbal *reactions* of the families to information that was new to them, if not to us. The scene became extremely moving and we cut fewer lines than is usual. Words are not the only means of communication in theatre. Shakespeare uses all the tools of dramaturgy, as I will continue to explore in the second half of this book.

At the end of this recounting, the Prince says, "And I, for winking at your discords, too, / Have lost a brace of kinsmen. All are punished."[27] A brace means *two* deaths in each of the three households: Romeo and his mother, Tybalt and Juliet, and Mercutio and Paris. The Montagues and the Capulets react in pain: the losses fall heavily on them. Their final words to each other are moving, but Shakespeare adds a pinch of salt to the wounds that the play inflicts on us, as they continue to compete with each other:

CAPULET
  O brother Montague, give me thy hand.
  This is my daughter's jointure, for no more
  Can I demand.
MONTAGUE   But I can give thee more;
  For I will ray her statue in pure gold,
  That whiles Verona by that name is known,
  There shall no figure at such rate be set,
  As that of true and faithful Juliet.
CAPULET
  As rich as Romeo's by his lady's lie,
  Poor sacrifices of our enmity.[28]

Montague and Capulet share a verse line to underline the reconciliation, but statues arrayed in pure gold? The use of the word "gold" seems pointed after Romeo's use of that word two short scenes earlier, and the addition of "pure" underscores its vulgarity. Shakespeare's endings are often more sophisticated than they at first appear. He likes to end with questions. Will Malcolm make a good king for Scotland? He has a streak of ruthlessness that he shares with Prince Hal. What happens to Prospero after he returns to Italy? He tells us every third thought will be of his death.

Love and power are the two great subjects of *Romeo and Juliet*. Shakespeare has already shown how sexual tensions and insecurities trap its young characters into the cycle of violence that consumes the families. Now, this remarkable play, which began with an argument over rank, ends with a reminder that the second source of that violence is the competition for status and power that money confers. Capulet's and Montague's lines should leave us to question what the heads of these families have learned.

Notes

1 *Romeo and Juliet*, ed. Jill L. Levenson (Oxford World's Classics, 2000), 1.2.24.
2 Ibid., 1.2.30–33.
3 Ibid., 1.4.229–30.
4 Ibid., 2.1.127.
5 Ibid., 2.6.32–34.
6 Ibid., 1.4.129–39.
7 Ibid., 4.4.54–55.
8 Stephen Greenblatt, *Will in the World* (Norton, 2004), Chapter 2. Greenblatt's excellent biography is brimming with pertinent descriptions of Shakespeare's world.
9 *Romeo and Juliet*, ed. Levenson, 1.1.76.
10 Ibid., 1.1.150–51.
11 Ibid., 5.3.211.
12 Des McAnuff's 1981 production for the New York Shakespeare Festival at the Delacorte Theatre in Central Park.
13 *Henry IV, Part One*, ed. A. R. Humphreys, Arden Second Series (Methuen, 1960), 2.4.41–48. This is the formatting for this Arden edition.
14 Ibid., 2.4.99–103. The now archaic use of *me* in this line, called the "ethic dative," can cause confusion today. It does not mean that Hotspur is killing Scots *for* the Prince. It is used to give emphasis to a past action. Drop the pronoun to achieve the sense.
15 *Romeo and Juliet*, ed. Levenson, 4.4.64–81.
16 Ibid., 4.4.97.
17 Ibid., 4.4.124–25.
18 *Shakespeare's Plays in Quarto*, eds. Michael J. B. Allen and Kenneth Muir (University of California Press, 1981), p. 195.
19 *Romeo and Juliet*, ed. Levenson, 4.4.136–45.
20 Ibid., 4.4.150, 160–61.
21 Ibid., 4.4.166.
22 *As You Like It*, ed. Alan Brissenden (Oxford World Classics, 1993), 4.3.176–177.
23 *The Tempest*, ed. Stephen Orgel (Oxford World's Classics, 1987), 4.1.156–58.
24 *Romeo and Juliet*, ed. Levenson, 5.1.37–54.
25 Ibid., 5.1.69–73.
26 Ibid., 5.1.80–83.
27 Ibid., 5.3.294–95.
28 Ibid., 5.3.296–97.

Bibliography

Shakespeare editions cited

As You Like It. Ed. Alan Brissenden. Oxford World Classics, 1993.

Henry IV, Part One. Ed. A. R. Humphreys. Arden Second Series. Methuen, 1960.

Romeo and Juliet. Ed. Jill L. Levenson. Oxford World's Classics, 2000.

Shakespeare's Plays in Quarto. Eds. Michael J. B. Allen and Kenneth Muir. University of California Press, 1981.

The Tempest. Ed. Stephen Orgel. Oxford World's Classics, 1987.

Other source

Greenblatt, Stephen. *Will in the World*. Norton, 2004.

Part II

Macbeth

Beyond the dialogue

7 Dramatic structure

As I turn to *Macbeth*, I will focus on elements of Shakespeare's dramaturgy that are often overlooked because they disappear on the page. Implied stage directions may be suggested in the dialogue. Silent characters may be key to a scene. The power of nonverbal reactions becomes apparent in the three dimensions of a rehearsal room when a director puts a scene on its feet. In the previous chapter, I cited an example from the end of *Romeo and Juliet*. Rosalind and Orlando's duets in the Forest of Arden provide another. They are actually trios. Celia becomes progressively more verbal in her disapproval of Rosalind's tactics in the sequence of these scenes, but even before she speaks up her silent reactions to Rosalind's tactics can also inform the way we perceive them.

In this half of the book, I will also examine how the relationship between actor and audience changes the function of words in soliloquies, and will explore the variety of ways that actions define a play. In *Macbeth*, choices matter, those made by the couple at the center of the play as well as the choices made by the members of the court.

I will begin by exploring how repeated actions create the dramatic structure of a play, and what we can learn about a play by examining its structure.

Parting is sweet sorrow

"Life without structure is unseen. Pure life expresses itself within and through structure."[1] I love this quote from John Cage. The composer best remembered for his principle of chance operation clearly sees structure as essential to his and other work. Structure is one way in which the content of a play is conveyed beyond the dialogue. The way events proceed – the shape of the play – is part of how we perceive it. A good writer organizes material so we can better understand what it contains. Novels lend themselves to an episodic structure because we rarely read a novel in one sitting.

In theatre, material must be organized in a way that maximizes our experience in one viewing. One way of doing that is through repetition.

I want to take a final look at *Romeo and Juliet* by examining its structure. That play, as previously mentioned, is anchored to a series of three public scenes that contain a large number of characters. These scenes are placed at the beginning, in the middle, and at the end of the play. Each ends with the entrance of the Prince: indeed, they are the only scenes where he speaks.[2] No one dies in the first scene, but the citizens lament the damage the brawl has caused. The second time this kind of sequence occurs Mercutio and Tybalt are killed. In the third sequence, Paris, Romeo, and Juliet die, and the death of Montague's Wife is announced.

To this pattern I would add two celebrations that are placed halfway between each of these three. Capulet's ball occurs halfway between the first two; Juliet's wedding party is halfway between the second and the third. Invitations are sent out for both. Both scenes are introduced by a flurry of preparations; both require musicians. The wedding doesn't proceed, of course, because the Capulets believe that Juliet is dead. The second party doesn't happen.

These five scenes, regularly interspersed, create a structure for the *public* story of the play. The fulcrum of the public story, the scene in which Mercutio and Tybalt are killed, is placed right in the middle. It changes everything. This structure is dramatic because the fights within them recur with an increasing number of deaths, and the party scenes move from celebration to mourning. There is change from parallel scene to parallel scene, and change (or the deliberate lack of it) is at the heart of drama:

first and last fight scenes	1.1				5.3
two party scenes		1.5		4.4	
middle fight scene, the fulcrum of the play			3.1		

Harry Levin points out that between the large scenes, "we shuttle through interiors, in a flurry of domestic arrangements and family relationships . . . the sphere of privacy encloses Acts II and IV, in contradistinction to the public issues raised elsewhere."[3] I would amend this by pointing out that these *private* stories invade all five acts of the play, largely in paired scenes, one in each half. These scenes are usually intimate duets or trios, which sets them apart visually from the large public scenes. There is a striking change in each of the paired scenes as well. Repeating similar scenes draws attention to what has changed and so advances the narrative. That is why repetition is so useful in playwriting and in text analysis. Capulet and Paris have two scenes on the subject of marriage to Juliet. In the first Paris presses an "elusive" Capulet for permission; in the second Capulet offers his daughter to him. Juliet has two scenes on the subject of marriage to Paris. In the first she cleverly avoids saying yes; in the second she says a definite no. There are actually two balcony scenes in the play. In the first Juliet and Romeo's marriage is proposed and they agree on the time and place. In the second, their marriage is consummated and they part not knowing when they will see each other again. There are also two Romeo/Friar scenes, and two Juliet/Nurse duets in which she awaits news about Romeo.

Each member of the pair is placed on either side of the fulcrum of the private story, the marriage. It changes everything. The pivotal scene in the public story, 3.1, follows it. They are literally at the center of the play. Shakespeare is using the five-act classical model for tragedy as it came down to the Elizabethans from the Roman playwright, Seneca, with the turning point in the middle of the play.

There are also scenes in the first half which are not repeated. They show us Romeo in the company of his friends. They cannot be repeated because Romeo is in the process of breaking away from them, as he is first preoccupied with Rosaline and then falls in love with Juliet. The absence of the pack, particularly of Mercutio, is deeply felt in the second half of the play, where these scenes are replaced by additional stage time for the Capulet household.

Structural analysis is most useful early in the examination of a play. It can help us size up a play – or a sequence of scenes, as we will explore later – from their outlines, before we invest the time required for detailed textual analysis. In *Romeo and Juliet*, it shows us very quickly that a large part of the text is devoted to a public story and that public story, as indicated in the sonnet that opens the play, must be taken into account. Structure also shows us that Romeo and his friends dominate the first half of the play, as he breaks away from them, and that Juliet and her family dominate the second, as she breaks away from them.

It also shows us that Romeo and Juliet gradually enter the play's public story, as Romeo is fatally drawn into the fight sequences *twice* despite his best intentions and Juliet is forced into a marriage to Paris because of her family's needs. The lovers are pulled into the public story of the play. Finally, it reveals that the second half of the play is a dark mirror of the comedic first half.

Structure is a fundamental tool of playwriting. It helps playwrights to chart the dramatic movement of a play and it helps audiences navigate through that play as they witness the changes in similar scenes. Few playwrights have Shakespeare's ability to infuse meaning into the form itself. *Romeo and Juliet* is an underrated play. It is not an early play: it is the work of a playwright who probably had a quarter of his career behind him. Audiences love this play because a compelling story is articulated through a dynamic structure.

Other structures

Aristotle wrote that the plot of a play is the arrangement of outward events that point to the inner actions from which they spring.[4] Structural analysis is a way of charting that *outward* arrangement, so that we can begin to deduce the inner actions, what I call the content. In the theater, that discovery is at the center of what we do in preparing for rehearsals and it continues throughout the rehearsal process and into performance, where the audience participates in that discovery.

The mirror is one dramatic structure. Aeschylus's *The Trojan Women* has another simple structure that embodies its story. After the fall of Troy, Queen Hecuba and her daughters are led off, one by one, to become concubines for their Greek victors. The parade of exits is intensified with finalities that cannot be reversed. Hecuba learns that one daughter has been sacrificed to the gods. Later her grandson is slaughtered as well. At the end, Hecuba and the chorus of the women of Troy exit the stage for servitude in exile. This is a dramatic pattern because Hecuba's pain increases as her family is torn apart, and the body of her grandson is brought onstage.

The dispersal of a family unit is an effective dramatic structure because of its simplicity and because we have an *emotional* relationship to it. Text analysis lends itself to intellectual observations, but we must never forget the emotional components of theatre. They are as important as the intellectual, and an important way by which the audience receives a play. Shakespeare is a master of landing emotional moments with minimum effort: "Thy lips are warm" and "Signifying nothing" are two examples. The film director Federico Fellini described his screenwriting process in this way in an interview: "I first try to express my own emotions, what I personally feel, and then I look for the link of truth that will make it of significance to people like me."[5]

The dispersal of a family is also the structure of Bertolt Brecht's *Mother Courage and Her Children*, as they struggle to make it through another brutal war. One by one her three children leave or die in virtually every other scene in the play. Its structure is breathtakingly simple. So that we do not see the pattern immediately, Brecht extends the characters to include Courage's two lovers, the Chaplain and the Cook, and for a time the prostitute, Yvette. They become part of the extended family and they too will leave: they become part of the dispersal. Courage's wagon is such a strong stage image because it helps us to see the depletion of the extended family, as a decreasing number of people pull it off, until she pulls it off alone at the end of the play.

Note that neither she nor we experience her losses in a linear way. The deaths of her sons, Swiss Cheese and Eilif, is more than the loss of two children, it is the pain of having lost *two* of your three children. The death of her only remaining child, her daughter Katrin, is heartbreaking. With each death, her pain increases *exponentially*. This occurs in *Romeo and Juliet* as well. In the three large public scenes, the number of deaths increases from none in the first, to two in the second, to four in the third.

The great American musical *Gypsy* also uses the dispersal of the family structure. Rose and her two daughters struggle to make it through the Depression. One child flees the domination of her mother at the end of Act One, but the decimation of the family unit is blurred by the addition of Rose's lover. The second-act trio, "Together," with its refrain, "Together wherever we go," is the perfect ironic anthem for this structure. In Act Two, the dispersal of the family accelerates. Rose's lover leaves and later her second child makes her exit as well, but in a sentimental moment returns at the end.

The structure of *Macbeth*

As I move into a consideration of *Macbeth* in the second half of this book, I want to begin by analyzing its narrative structure. Look for patterns in the *narrative* of the play, the repeated events. After identifying the patterns of the events, you can then proceed to identify what the structure tells us about the inner action of the play: if drama is defined by change, what are the changes from like scene to like scene?

What are the major events in the plot of *Macbeth*? There are a series of murders. Duncan is murdered, then Banquo, and then Lady Macduff and her family. If we accept the five-act structure of the Folio, then these murders take place in the middle three acts of the play. These murders are usually preceded by scenes in which they are planned, and followed by scenes in which the murders are announced. These are the obvious observations, but the middle acts share something else. Each ends with what I call a choral scene in which Scottish thanes lament these deaths and open the narrative to the public story: their effect on Scotland. Note that I have added 1.7 to the pattern of the middle acts to chart the repetitions in this way:

1.7:	Macbeth/Wife plan	*3.1*:	Macb/Murds plan	*4.1*:	Macbeth decides alone; no one ruminates
2.1:	Macbeth ruminates	*3.2*:	Macbeth/Wife ruminate		
2.2:	Duncan is murdered; his sons flee	*3.3*:	Banquo is murdered; his son barely escapes	*4.2*:	Duff's family murdered; no children escape
2.3:	murder is announced	*3.4*:	murder is reported	*4.3*:	murders reported
2.4:	Ross/Macduff lament	*3.6*:	Lennox/Lord lament		Malcolm/Duff lament

The differences from like scene to like scene tell us much about the play. Macbeth begins to make decisions by himself and eventually, and dangerously, instantaneously. The murders become more horrific as they begin to occur onstage and *children* progressively become targets. As the murders multiply, the lords in the choral scenes move into exile and action that carries us into Act Five.

What are the events in Act Five? Scenes involving Macbeth and his court alternate with scenes with those who would overthrow it. English forces led by Malcolm invade from the south and meet up with rebels who have gathered in Scotland to oppose Macbeth. Where have we seen this pattern before? In Act One Duncan fights forces from inside and outside Scotland as well, a rebellion led by the Scot, Macdonald, and an invasion from the north led by the King of Norway and supported by Cawdor.

The alternating actions of the outer acts can be charted in this way:

	5.1: Lady Macbeth exits play
1.1: Weïrd Sisters	*5.2*: Scottish opposition
1.2: Duncan's court	*5.3*: Macbeth's court
1.3: Weïrd Sisters	*5.4*: Scottish opposition
1.4: Duncan's court	*5.5*: Macbeth's court
1.5: Lady Macbeth enters play	*5.6–end*: Scottish opposition:
1.6: Duncan's court enters castle	Malcolm's court enters castle

The structure of Acts One and Five are strikingly similar to each other and strikingly different from the middle three acts of the play. In *Romeo and Juliet*, the public and the private stories alternate. In *Macbeth*, three acts of murder are bookended by two acts of civil war and invasion. The outer acts focus more on a public story that includes war and the naming of a king. In Act One, Macbeth is named as Thane of Cawdor and Malcolm as Duncan's heir. In Act Five, the thanes are named earls and Malcolm becomes king.

The middle three acts focus on the murders and, apart from the choral scenes, the private stories of two couples – the Macbeths in Acts Two and Three and the Macduffs in Act Four. Anthony Brennan points out that Lady Macbeth literally enters the play 292 lines into it and exits from the play 291 lines from the end, which defines the middle section of the play.[6]

Into the woods

Shakespeare used some version of Macbeth's structure in at least a quarter of his plays. It allowed him to examine both public and private stories, but to separate them in a different way from the mirror structure. The public story is set up in the first act. The middle acts largely focus on progressive change in the private stories that leads to a change in the public story in the final act. You can see it in its purest form in one of its earliest incarnations in Shakespeare – *A Midsummer Night's Dream*. The problems of an everyday sometimes corrupt world, usually urban or court-centered, are explored and sometimes resolved in a rural, often exotic, and sometimes magical other world. This is the outline of the pastoral romances that were being imported from Italy to England at this time. In *Midsummer*, the outer acts take place in the public world of Athens, and the middle three acts in the woods. Lives are rearranged in the woods through the intervention of the fairies. The resolution of the public story, the relationship between Theseus and Hippolyta, begins when they encounter the lovers in the woods at the end of Act Four, and Theseus accepts the couplings that he rejected at the beginning of the play. In Act Five, all celebrate back at the court.

As You Like It also begins in the cruel world of a court, before its characters enter the Forest of Arden, but here there is an important advancement in Shakespeare's art. The "magic" of these woods is not in an outside agent such as the fairies, but in what his characters learn about themselves. As in *Midsummer*, life in the "other" world is not ideal, and those who remain there do not change. Jacques remains in the forest to pursue his dream of an ideal life, but so do Silvius and Phoebe, to remind us what the reality of life is there. The other characters return to the court at the end, but Shakespeare brings the play to a close before they do. The bookend structure is implied, but we do not witness it, so that the play can end as a comedy. What happens after his lovers reenter the everyday world, Shakespeare keeps to himself. *A Winter's Tale* also begins in a corrupt court before its pastoral respite in Bohemia.

One of Shakespeare's earliest plays provides an interesting prototype. The two gentlemen of Verona journey from life in a small town to the big city of Milan, which is as exotic for them as London must have been for a country boy like Shakespeare. Later, when Shakespeare moved to the big city, the exotic other world became a romanticized version of the countryside of his youth, which literally contained a Forest of Arden, outside of Stratford.

In three plays that involve shipwrecks, the entire play takes place in that exotic other world. Another early play provides the prototype. In *The Comedy of Errors*, the boys from Syracuse – a father and two sets of sons (and rarely in Shakespeare, also a mother) – are reunited in an exotic city where mad things seem to happen. In *Twelfth Night*, Viola and Sebastian are shipwrecked in a foreign country populated by people maddened by love. "Doctors" appear in both, couples are rearranged, but only in the last of the three do they go back. In *The Tempest*, Prospero lands on a magical island, far from the cruelties he has experienced in the courts of Italy. Like Rosalind, he has been forced into exile, but once there he repeats the mistakes of the past. Prospero's new world is the familiar old one, in which a master rules and subjects must obey. He understands, as his daughter does not, that the creatures from the "brave new world" are part of a corrupt old one, but he will return there with his daughter because he loves her.

The flexibility of this structure allows Shakespeare its use in tragedies as well. *Othello* moves to the exotic frontier of Cyprus from the "civilized" court of Venice, which reasserts itself at the end when the Venetians reappear. *Macbeth* has this "Into the Woods" structure as well, but here the often dreamlike state of the place of retreat has become, to use Jan Kott's word, a full-fledged "nightmare."[7] Once the characters cross the threshold of Macbeth's castle, they do not return to full daylight until the last scene of Act Four. It is an extremely regular play that lends itself to structural analysis.

Structural analysis works because dramatic structure charts the internal rhythm of a play, the repetitions that we first only vaguely sense and then may even anticipate as we begin to recognize the patterns that the playwright lays out before us. You do not need to understand all the implications of structure at once. Some may be immediately apparent; some will become clear only as you move into a text analysis of the play, as we will do now with *Macbeth*.

Notes

1 John Cage from "Lecture on Nothing," 1949, in the collection *Silence* (Wesleyan University Press, 1961), p. 133.
2 The interior structure of these scenes is further detailed at the end of Chapter One.
3 Harry Levin, "Form and Formality in 'Romeo and Juliet'," in *Shakespeare and the Revolution of the Times* (Galaxy, 1976), pp. 110–11.
4 Francis Fergusson, " 'Macbeth' as the Imitation of an Action," in *Essays in Shakespearean Criticism*, eds. James L. Calderwood and Harold E. Toliver (Prentice Hall, 1970), p. 514.
5 Charlotte Chandler, *I, Fellini* (Random House, 1995), p. 147.
6 Anthony Brennan, *Shakespeare's Dramatic Structures* (Routledge, 1986), p. 120.
7 Jan Kott, *Shakespeare Our Contemporary* (Norton, 1964), pp. 85–86. Kott's book contains the quintessential essay on Shakespeare's histories, which he then uses as a point of departure for chapters on the major tragedies, including an important essay on *Macbeth*.

Bibliography

Brennan, Anthony. *Shakespeare's Dramatic Structures*. Routledge, 1986.
Cage, John. "Lecture on Nothing" (1949). From the collection *Silence*. Wesleyan University Press, 1961.
Chandler, Charlotte. *I, Fellini*. Random House, 1995.

Fergusson, Francis. "'Macbeth' as the Imitation of an Action." In *Essays in Shakespearean Criticism*, eds. James L. Calderwood and Harold E. Toliver. Prentice Hall, 1970, pp. 513–520.

Kott, Jan. *Shakespeare Our Contemporary*. Norton, 1964.

Levin, Harry. "Form and Formality in 'Romeo and Juliet'." In *Shakespeare and the Revolution of the Times*. Galaxy, 1976.

8 English history in the Scottish Play

When we work on a new play, we read the script and discuss it with the writer. The focus is naturally on the text. In working on classics, we often turn to secondary writings after reading the script. I chose to examine *Macbeth* in part because research is necessary to understanding this dense, complex play. Secondary reading comes in two modes: knowledge and opinions. Opinions have value, even when we disagree with them, because they can help define the key issues in a play. Turning to opinions too soon, however, can prescribe your own response to the plays. Later, when your head is full of the opinions of others, it may be important to remember what struck you in your first readings.

Knowledge, on the other hand, is essential when approaching plays that are 400 years old. Shakespeare's plays are often reduced to character studies because his observations about English society, observations that his original audiences would have immediately recognized, may be difficult for us to discern today. The tension between old landed money and the rising merchant class that fuels *Romeo and Juliet* is one example. Recently I have witnessed how good productions have reduced the full scope of Shakespeare's plays by ignoring such conflicts in them. Public stories that still have value for us today disappeared, and the private stories were oversimplified as a result.

There are three time periods that are essential to understanding Shakespeare's plays: the environment in which Shakespeare wrote his plays, the period in which we live, and that between the writing of the plays and the present. In this chapter, we will examine the first of them.

"What are you?"

When Macbeth first meets the "Weïrd Sisters," he asks the question: "What are you?"[1]

The answer to that question would seem simple. The play begins with these words: "*Thunder and Lightning. Enter three Witches*."[2] Their presentation in the play, however, is more ambiguous than is often acknowledged. In his book *Shakespeare and Co.*, Stanley Wells cites an account by Simon Forman of a production he saw at the Globe in 1611. He describes the Sisters as "'Nimphes' who are encountered in a wood."[3] The validity of that description has been challenged, but it should alert us not to take for granted who the Sisters are in the play.

The Sisters are called "witches" in the Folio's stage directions, but in their speech prefixes, they are simply named 1, 2, and 3, although more complete designations are used for Banquo's "Murtherers" in 3.1 (1 Murth. and 2 Murth.) and for the Apparitions in the cauldron scene (1 Appar., 2 Appar., 3 Appar., etc.).[4] The exception is the short scene in which Banquo is murdered, where the designation of the murderers is also numeric. In the dialogue of the play, however, the Sisters refer to each other only as "sister" and collectively as the "Weïrd Sisters." Elsewhere, Macbeth refers to them as the "Weïrd Sisters," and Banquo calls them the "Weïrd Women."[5] The only time "witch" is *spoken* in the play is as a disparagement. In their second scene, a sea-captain's wife tells the First Sister to get lost – "Aroynt thee, witch" – when she asks the wife for some of the food that she is eating.[6]

The word "weïrd" itself does not occur in the Folio, the only authoritative text we have for a play that has no extant quartos. "Weïrd" is an emendation by an early editor, Theobald, who made the change in 1734. In the Folio, the terms used are "Weyward" or "Weyard" Sisters. Theobald may have taken "weïrd" from Raphael Holinshed's *Chronicles of Scotland*, one of Shakespeare's chief sources for the play: "the common opinion was, that these women were either the weïrd sisters, that is (as ye would say) the goddesses of destinie, or else some nymphs or feiries, indued with knowledge of prophesie by their necromanticall [sic] science."[7]

The appearance of Hecate, the Greek goddess of witchcraft, in 3.5 and 4.1 would seem to confirm that the Sisters are witches, but her scenes are seldom seen today because it is now generally agreed that they were added after the original performances. Both 3.5 and Hecate's lines in 4.1 are written in iambic meter rather than the predominantly trochaic meter of the Sisters elsewhere. The contradictory reports in 3.6 and 4.1 about when Macbeth learns that Macduff has fled to England may have been the result of "working sheets of a revision not finally tidied up for performance" to include Hecate.[8] In addition, two songs that appear in the Hecate scenes are indicated only by quoting their first lines, something which is not done elsewhere in the Folio. These songs appear in full in Thomas Middleton's play *The Witch*, and Middleton is now considered the favorite candidate as author or co-author of the Hecate material in *Macbeth*.[9]

Collaboration was frequent in an Elizabethan and Jacobean theatre that generated so many plays. Wells discusses this in his book, as does James Shapiro in *Contested Will*, the definitive rebuttal to those who believe that

Shakespeare was not the author of the plays that the Folio credits to him.[10] Some co-authorship, however, is a different matter. Middleton may have apprenticed with Shakespeare and is now posited as the probable co-author of *Timon of Athens*. Nicolas Brooke believes that Hecate was added when Shakespeare was still active as a playwright, and argues both for Shakespeare as co-author of her scenes and the inclusion of those scenes in production.[11] In his excellent chapters on *Macbeth* in *The Year of Lear*, James Shapiro argues for a later date that makes it less likely that Shakespeare was co-author:

> It may be that Middleton, revisiting Shakespeare's play a decade or so after it was first staged [in 1606], felt that *Macbeth* wanted to be a devil play, or playgoers wanted it to be one. . . . There's no question that the inclusion of Middleton's songs and of the Hecate material tilts what Shakespeare likely first wrote in the direction of a play in which the supernatural holds sway.[12]

These Hecate additions, the play's brevity (perhaps the result of cuts), and the many sound cues in the play point to prompt-book copy as the source of the text. If so, the stage directions that contain the word "witch" may be the words of a book-keeper who assembled the revisions, perhaps even after Shakespeare's death in 1616. So are the Sisters weïrd or wayward, fates, nymphs, or witches? Their most impressive power, the conjuring of spirits to make predictions, usually belongs to the loftier realm of "necromancers," rather than that of common witches.[13]

These contradictions are reflected in current scholarship on the concept of witchcraft in Shakespeare's England. James I wrote a book on the subject called *Demonologie* (1597). His interest in witchcraft and the presence of a Scot on the throne are cited as the reasons Shakespeare turned to this story after James became king in 1603. It is usually assumed that all English people shared his belief. Stephen Greenblatt offers a more complex view in his 1993 essay, "Shakespeare Bewitched."[14] His research debunks any notions that the Catholic Church had a single position on the subject, detailing conflicting arguments within the Church about the existence of witches over centuries. The *Malleus malificarum*, written by two Dominican inquisitors in 1484, stated that it was heretical to deny the existence of witchcraft; Reginald Scot wrote that belief in witchcraft was delusional in a widely read book, *The Discoverie of Witchcraft*, written just twenty years before Shakespeare wrote *Macbeth*. King James's book was written in part to refute Scot.

In his essay, Greenblatt argues for a Jacobean society with differing views on the existence of the supernatural, not unlike the range of opinions on that subject that exists today. Did Shakespeare believe in witchcraft? Evidence in his plays is contradictory. Perhaps Shakespeare was ambivalent about the belief, or perhaps as Greenblatt suggests Shakespeare just acknowledged "the deeply contradictory ideological situation of his time (which has) haunted virtually all attempts to determine the status of witchcraft beliefs and practices."[15]

William C. Carroll seconds this point of view in the excellent contextual essays in the Bedford/St. Martin edition of the play:

> The discourse of witchcraft intersected with many other controversial issues of the time, from the place of women and the nature of supernatural power, to treason and regicide. It is impossible to specify what Shakespeare's audience in 1605–06 "believed" about witchcraft. Clearly, though, they did not all believe the same thing.[16]

I am not arguing that the Sisters were not witches in Shakespeare's mind. We have no way of knowing that, but we live in a post-Freudian age that is interested in motivation. Shakespeare was more interested in the *actions* that we take and the results of those actions. What is important about the Sisters is not who they are, but how they *affect* those they meet.

I would propose that the Sisters' ambiguity has actually been a gift to those who have produced the play. It has allowed the Sisters to endure through 400 years of changing ideas on the supernatural and filter the Sisters through the belief systems of our own times. I have worked on one production that saw them as practitioners of an earlier pagan religion, what we would call white witchcraft today.[17] Another presented them as spirits of the battlefield who ushered the dead offstage throughout the play.[18] Each time Macbeth meets them in Akira Kurosawa's great film adaptation *Throne of Blood* (1957) they appear in different manifestations, perhaps to represent the different aspects of their identity in the play.

Whatever they are, Shakespeare typically gives actors detail to help them differentiate their characters even within their short scenes. The excerpts below are from the Folio, where their speech designations are simply 1, 2 and 3. The rhythm of the Sisters' lines and their use of rhyme set them apart from the other characters of the play, but it is considerably varied in their early scenes. They usually speak in trochaic tetrameter that omits the unstressed syllable at the end. The play opens with such a trochaic line from the First Sister, here taken from the Folio:

```
      /    –    /  –     /  –   /
1: When shall | we three | meet a | gaine?   trochaic
```

For her second line, however, Shakespeare has the First Sister revert to iambic cadence:

– / – / – / – /
In Thun | der, Light | ning, or in | Raine? *iambic*

The First Sister takes the lead and drives the dialogue, here and elsewhere. The Second Sister responds with trochaic lines, but the third does not. Her meter in her early scenes is usually iambic. Here they begin with a trochee:

/ – – / – / – /
3: That will | be ere | the set | of Sunne . . .
/ – / – – /
There to | meet with | Mac beth.[19]

In the opening of their second scene, Shakespeare uses varying rhythms to give an exciting shape to their dialogue. After the initial questions, the First Sister's lines are largely iambic because her answer is in the casual mode of a narrative. She talks about her encounter with a sea-captain's well-fed wife, who is munching on chestnuts but refuses to share them, and dismisses her by calling the First Sister a witch. At this point the rhythm of the lines begins to change. They become shorter; a rhyme is introduced. The First Sister then hits dynamic rhythmic stride with a series of trochaic lines. The other Sisters offer to help her take revenge and join her for last lines of this section, which ends with, "Peace, the charm's wound up."[20]

Why does Shakespeare take the time to tell this story? Certainly it warns us that the Sisters can be dangerous when provoked, but the details of Shakespeare's imagery proffer more. The wife is described as well-fed, and the First Sister demands some of the food she is eating. When she refuses, the First Sister promises to take revenge by making her husband "dwindle, peak [become emaciated], and pine [suffering caused by hunger]."[21] Shakespeare is a good dramatist: here (and elsewhere) he lists a progression that advances the image. Banquo will use the same imagery when he describes the Sisters as "withered."[22] Taken together, Shakespeare presents us with a bleak picture of both their situation and that of the war-torn country.

Macbeth and Banquo now enter, and the Sisters address them boldly with the familiar pronoun. The First Sister takes the lead as usual, but tells Macbeth nothing new: "hail to thee Thane of Glamis!" The Second Sister hails him as the "Thane of Cawdor," an honor that was bestowed on Macbeth in the previous scene, but something he does not yet know. Only the Third Sister actually speaks about the future: "All hail Macbeth, that shall be King hereafter." She is the only one of the three who consistently makes predictions, here and elsewhere. To Banquo she says, "Thou shalt get kings, though thou be none."[23] In retrospect we can see that she also does this in scene one: "That will be ere the set of sun."[24] In this scene as in the first, she speaks in iambs. The Applause edition of the play puts it this way: "Notice how the Third Witch never matches the ritual speaking of the others throughout the scene."[25] Des presented her as an apprentice for this reason, even if a natural talent in terms of her ability to predict. It is not until the cauldron scene that she speaks largely in the trochaic cadence of the other Sisters.

If the First Sister can be seen as the leader and Third Sister is the apprentice who has the gift of foreknowledge, how would we characterize the Second Sister? In some versions of the Fates, as the Weïrd Sisters were represented in the source material – the Scandinavian Norns, for example – they represent the past, the present, and the future. Shakespeare may be playing off this. The domain of the First Sister, their leader and the most experienced, is the past (Glamis); the Second Sister's domain is the present (Cawdor), and the Third the future (King).

Detail for actors is characteristic of Shakespeare, even in small parts. Samson and Gregory are differentiated. The two murderers who kill Banquo are differentiated in their scene with Macbeth. One is reluctant and must be persuaded. The other is not, and the dynamics of the scene are built around that difference. The persuasion of the reluctant is a recurring dynamic in *Macbeth*, beginning with Macbeth and his wife. It continues throughout the play, culminating in 4.3, where Malcolm pretends to be reluctant to test Macduff.

At the beginning of the scene in which he meets the Sisters, Macbeth challenges them with "What are you?" – a question that is given a surprising twist in the Porter scene. After they make their predictions, he asks them to "Stay, you imperfect speakers."[26] By the end of the play, however, they have become "Juggling fiends . . . that palter us in a *double sense* [italics added]," and Macbeth berates them: "Th'equivocation of the fiend / That lies like truth."[27] That word, *equivocation*, is used for the first time in the play in the Porter scene, and had a highly charged and specific meaning in the period in which Shakespeare wrote *Macbeth*.

"Come in, equivocator"

The words *equivocator* and *equivocate* are used five times in the Porter scene. Today we more frequently use a related word, *equivocal*, which is defined in the *OED* as "capable of double interpretation; ambiguous." *Equivocate* is more narrowly defined: double interpretation *by intent*, in the language of the *OED*, "to mean one thing and express another . . . to prevaricate."[28] This word was famously used in a notorious trial that took place at the time of the writing of *Macbeth*. The date of this trial has been used to date the play.

In November of 1605 Guy Fawkes was discovered in a vault beneath Parliament. He was part of a plot by dissident Catholics to blow up the government when the King presided over the opening of Parliament. Catholics were forbidden the practice of their religion; their lands had been confiscated, and even harboring a priest was an offence punishable by death. Fawkes and a dozen co-conspirators were tried and hanged, drawn, and quartered in January. Some scholars have even suggested that the detailed description of the treachery and execution of Cawdor was a portrait of a conspirator whom King James knew personally, and who repented and died with dignity.

The Gunpowder Conspiracy, as it was called, reopened an old wound. Decades of concern about royal succession, precipitated by a childless queen, were alleviated with James I's accession to the throne. This issue is reflected in the number of children we find in a play that has a childless couple at its center, and the parade of kings in the cauldron scene that stretches "to th' crack of doom."[29] Now, the English public suddenly faced the near assassination of their new King and his entire government. Rumors of repeated attempts on the King's life followed, throwing London into periodic hysteria that may have inspired Ross' lines:

> But cruel are the times . . . when we hold rumour
> From what we fear, yet do not know what we fear,
> But float upon a wild and violent sea.[30]

James Shapiro describes the Gunpowder Conspiracy *and* its aftermath in vivid detail in *The Year of Lear*.[31] The Jesuit Superior for England, Henry Garnet, was put on trial that spring. One of the conspirators told Garnet about the plot in confession. Although he testified that he tried to dissuade the conspirators, he was convicted for not revealing the plot. During the trial, Garnet was asked about his treatise on the Jesuit doctrine of equivocation. It was the Jesuit view that Catholics could justifiably *mislead* Protestant inquisitors. One way was to give responses that contained an alternate, hidden meaning so that technically they were not lying. One could equivocate to protect one's religion. Shakespeare put the phrase "committed treason enough, for God's sake, yet could not equivocate to Heaven" into the mouth of the Porter.[32] Garnet was executed in May 1606, and his execution has been used to date *Macbeth*.

Shakespeare was clearly attracted to the story of Macbeth because a Scottish king was on the throne of England, but the Gunpowder Conspiracy and Garnet's trial made that story the perfect vehicle for examining an England that was now suddenly thrown into a state of fear by the near-murder of its king.

Shakespeare also reveals in the consequences of equivocation the costs of murder for those who commit it.

Notes

1 *Macbeth*, ed. Nicholas Brooke (Oxford World Classics, 1994), 1.3.47.
2 *The Norton Facsimile: The First Folio of Shakespeare*, ed. Charlton Hinman (Norton, 1968), p. 739.
3 Stanley Wells, *Shakespeare and Co.* (Pantheon, 2006), p. 190. Wells gives excellent summaries the work of Shakespeare's fellow playwrights, their influence of on each other, and their possible collaborations with Shakespeare.
4 The Norton Facsimile, ed. Charlton Hinman, 1–2–3: pp. 739–40 and 751–52; 1–2 *Murth.*: pp. 747–49; 1–3 *Appar.*: p. 752.
5 *Macbeth*, ed. Nicholas Brooke, Sister: 1.3.1 and 3; Weïrd Sisters: 1.3.32; 1.5.7–8, 3.4.134, 4.1.151; Weïrd Women: 3.1.2.
6 Ibid., 1.3.6.
7 *Macbeth*, ed. Kenneth Muir, Arden Second Series (Methuen, 1951), pp. 171–72. Excerpts from Holinshed's *Chronicles of Scotland.*
8 *Macbeth*, ed. Nicholas Brooke, p. 52.
9 Stanley Wells, *Shakespeare and Co.* (Pantheon, 2006), pp. 189–90.
10 James Shapiro, *Contested Will: Who Wrote Shakespeare*? (Simon & Schuster, 2010), pp. 254–59.
11 *Macbeth*, ed. Nicholas Brooke, pp. 51–56.
12 James Shapiro, *The Year of Lear* (Simon and Schuster, 2015), p. 193. In this excellent book, Shapiro also provides historical context for two other plays, *Lear* and *Antony and Cleopatra*.
13 Henry N. Paul, *The Royal Play of Macbeth* (Macmillan, 1950), p. 270.
14 Stephen Greenblatt, "Shakespeare Bewitched," in *New Historical Literary Study*, eds. Jeffrey N. Cox and Larry J. Reynolds (Princeton, 1993).
15 Ibid., p. 123.
16 *Macbeth*, ed. William C. Carroll (Bedford/St. Martin's, 1999), p. 306. The editions of the plays in this incomplete series offer extensive historical material that places the plays in context of their times.
17 Des McAnuff's production at the La Jolla Playhouse in 1989.
18 Moises Kaufman's 2006 production in Central Park for New York's Public Theater.
19 The Norton Facsimile, ed. Charlton Hinman, p. 739.
20 *Macbeth*, ed. Nicholas Brooke, 1.3.37.
21 Ibid., 1.3.23.
22 Ibid., 1.3.40.
23 Ibid., 1.3.48–50 and 1.3.68.
24 Ibid., 1.1.5.

25 *Macbeth*, ed. Neil Freeman (Applause, 2000), p. 1, note 2.
26 *Macbeth*, ed. Nicholas Brooke, 1.3.47 and 70.
27 Ibid., 5.7.49–50 and 5.5.43–44.
28 *Oxford English Dictionary* (Oxford University Press, 1971), equivocal: 2; equivocate: 4
29 *Macbeth*, ed. Nicholas Brooke, 4.1.132.
30 Ibid., 4.2.18–21.
31 James Shapiro, *The Year of Lear* (Simon and Schuster, 2015).
32 *Macbeth*, ed. Nicholas Brooke, 2.3.9–11.

Bibliography

Shakespeare editions cited

Macbeth. Ed. Kenneth Muir, Arden Second Series. Methuen, 1951.
Macbeth. Ed. Neil Freeman. Applause, 2000.
Macbeth. Ed. Nicholas Brooke. Oxford World Classics, 1994.
Macbeth. Ed. William C. Carroll. Bedford/St. Martin's, 1999.
The Norton Facsimile: *The First Folio of Shakespeare*. Ed. Charlton Hinman. Norton, 1968.

Other sources

Greenblatt, Stephen. "Shakespeare Bewitched." In *New Historical Literary Study*, eds. Jeffrey N. Cox and Larry J. Reynolds. Princeton University Press, 1993, pp. 108–135.
Oxford English Dictionary. Oxford University Press, 1971.
Paul, Henry. *The Royal Play of Macbeth*. Macmillan, 1950.
Shapiro, James. *Contested Will: Who Wrote Shakespeare*? Simon & Schuster, 2010.
Shapiro, James. *The Year of Lear*. Simon and Schuster, 2015.
Wells, Stanley. *Shakespeare and Co*. Pantheon, 2006.

9 Mr. and Mrs. Macbeth

In this chapter I will focus on the private story, the extraordinary relationship between husband and wife that is at the center of Shakespeare's play. Shakespeare takes us on one of the darkest rides in theatre, and part of the terror he creates is achieved by forcing us to experience much of the first two acts of the play through his two leads. What allowed him to do this was his mastery of the soliloquy in the series of great tragedies that began with *Hamlet*.

Anthony Brennan points out that "some 260 lines, over a tenth of the play, are devoted to soliloquies and asides and all but thirty of these lines are given to Macbeth and his wife."[1] Shakespeare puts us inside the heads of the Macbeths through their many asides and soliloquies. This creates a bond with the audience that, as we will see, Shakespeare continues to manipulate throughout the play.

Enter Macbeth and Banquo

Macbeth is often presented in production as the embodiment of evil from the beginning of the play, but this is not what we find in the text. Before we meet him, Macbeth is described as a war hero who saves his country from the dual disaster of domestic rebellion and foreign invasion. This and his early struggles with his "black and deep desires"[2] allow us to enter his journey with him rather than against him.

When we first meet him, it is Banquo who dominates the *dialogue*. Macbeth is a man of few words – two lines among the first thirty – and intense thoughts that are expressed in this scene in his many asides and a long soliloquy. Indeed, he is not in a scene where he has most of the *dialogue* until Act Three, where he has begun to change following the first murder.

In 1.3, his first reaction to the Sisters' predictions is silence. Banquo describes his expression: "Good sir, why do you start, and seem to fear / Things that do sound so fair?"[3] What he is thinking Shakespeare withholds from us for the moment, but soon he gives us the first indication. When the

Wayward Sisters start to leave, Macbeth asks them to "Stay, you imperfect speakers, tell me more."[4]

Ross enters and Macbeth responds to the news that Duncan has named him Thane of Cawdor with a few lines and a long soliloquy that begins, "Two truths are told / As happy prologues to the swelling act / Of the imperial theme."[5] This remarkable soldier is also an exceptional poet. His soliloquy builds to the word *murder* at the end, one of the few times he uses that word in the play. He immediately qualifies it by saying that his "thought" is "but fantastical."[6] A few lines later he backs away from even that: "If chance will have me King, why chance may crown me, / Without my stir."[7]

There is an interesting change in the tone of Macbeth's language, when he comes out of this reverie to address Banquo, Ross, and Angus. He uses a formality of language that he has not previously displayed:

> Give me your favour: my dull brain was wrought
> With things forgotten. Kind gentlemen, your pains
> Are registered where every day I turn
> The leaf to read them. Let us toward the King.[8]

"Things forgotten" refers to thoughts of murder that Macbeth has temporarily abandoned, but he knows that is not the way Banquo, Ross, and Angus will take it. This is a significant moment for the actor playing Macbeth. He is *equivocating* for the first time in the play. Macbeth has deliberately put on a mask to hide his thoughts, and this change to what is for him an artificial-sounding language signals his deception. "Hear not my steps," he says later as he moves towards Duncan's chamber to murder him.[9] Shakespeare shows us Macbeth's descent into evil, step by step. He will move inevitably towards murder, even as he continually tries to talk himself out of it.

Nuance in language is often difficult to spot four hundred years later, and it is important to note that when they meet for the first time in the play, Duncan greets Macbeth with extravagant, public speech and Macbeth reciprocates in kind:

DUNCAN . . . O worthiest cousin,
The sin of my ingratitude even now
Was heavy on me. Thou art so far before
That swiftest wing of recompense is slow
To overtake thee . . . only I have left to say,
More is thy due, than more than all can pay.
MACBETH
The service and the loyalty that I owe,
In doing it, pays itself.
Your highness' part, is to receive our duties;

And our duties are to your throne and state,
Children and servants, which do but what they should
By doing everything safe towards your love
And honour.
DUNCAN Welcome hither:
I have begun to plant thee, and will labour
To make thee full of growing . . .[10]

Do we assign this inflated language to the nature of the occasion, to political posturing, or both? Duncan must carefully praise his war hero before this assembly of thanes. After all, Macbeth saved Scotland from the dual threats that Duncan was not able to prevent or contain. Having rejected murder on the hope that "chance may crown me," Macbeth now expresses his loyalty to Duncan's throne and state, which gives the King an easy segue to the naming of his son the Prince of Cumberland, that is, Duncan's successor. Shakespeare is a master of creating forward movement in dialogue. One line leads to another, sometimes, as here, unexpectedly.

At this time, Scottish kingship was in a period of transition to lineal succession. Traditionally the King was chosen by a group of closely related thanes from among their ranks, and usually the position went to their chief warrior. Though a few early passages such as this and the one below suggest that Shakespeare may have known about *tanistry*, as it was called, he does not mention it explicitly in his play, perhaps because to do so would give a slighted Macbeth an excuse for his actions.

The scene ends with Macbeth's comment on this announcement:

The Prince of Cumberland: that is a step
On which I must fall down, or else o'er-leap,
For in my way it lies. Stars hide your fires,
Let not light see my black and deep desires,
The eye wink at the hand – yet let that be
Which the eye fears, when it is done, to see.[11]

In this remarkable soliloquy, Macbeth asks for the assistance of night to hide his "black and deep desires." His wife will also beckon night in the next scene. Her soliloquy will usher in the long middle of the play, which largely takes place indoors, at dusk, night, or in murky daylight. Here, Macbeth asks for something else that is important to our understanding of his character. "Let . . . the eye wink at the hand" betrays his need for another kind of equivocation – the need to deceive him*self*, so he cannot see himself committing the terrible act of murder. This is another step on his way to committing it.

Shakespeare is at the summit of his narrative powers in *Macbeth*, and its glorious language is seldom discursive. One of his shortest plays, *Macbeth* is so terse and moves forward with such velocity, that you must ensure that the audience registers the significant details such as those above, or its inexorable logic will derail. This is the real "curse" of *Macbeth* that makes mounting it with complete success so difficult.

"Enter Macbeths wife Alone with a letter"[12]

Lady Macbeth is contrasted to her husband from the beginning and their scenes are driven by this difference. Macbeth is slow to reveal himself, a reflective man whose interior debates regularly stop him in his tracks and prevent him from taking action. We do not see that struggle in his wife: "I feel now / The future in the instant."[13] Lady Macbeth begins her first scene in prose because prose is the convention for the letter she is reading. We meet her in unguarded private thoughts, and in contrast to her husband's first scene she speaks all but eight lines. Her many monosyllabic words and trochees give her speech vigor. Their intimacy is set up by his reference to her in his letter as "my dearest partner of greatness,"[14] and she uses the familiar *thou* when referring to her husband, rather than the deferential formality of *you,* which was customary for wife to husband at this time.

The imagery in the soliloquy that follows ("unsex me here") is so ferocious that it is easy to overlook that it is an active speech: even Lady Macbeth must fortify herself in order to commit the terrible act of murder. She echoes her husband's line about letting "the eye wink at the hand" when she asks for Night to cover itself "in the dunnest smoke of Hell, / That my keen knife see not the wound it makes."[15]

Macbeth enters and addresses her with affection, calling her "My dearest love" and later, "love," "dear wife," and "dearest chuck."[16] She, in turn, addresses him by his titles, "Great Glamis! worthy Cawdor," and "My Thane," in their first scene. Sadly, she calls him simply "sir" in their last scene, when their relationship has deteriorated.[17] She never talks about what the murder will mean for her: she focuses on what it will mean for him. At the heart of this dark ride is a love story. It is this vestige of their humanity that should continue to move us throughout the play. Stephen Greenblatt writes in his biography of Shakespeare: "There are two significant exceptions to [his] unwillingness or inability to imagine a married couple in a relationship of sustained intimacy, but they are unnervingly strange: Gertrude and Claudius in *Hamlet* and the Macbeths."[18]

Lady Macbeth doesn't use the word *murder* when they first meet in the play. Perhaps they have discussed it before; perhaps she understands how difficult that idea is for him. They inhabit each other's minds so completely they do not speak that word, and their shared lines here reinforce this intimacy. They *do* need to look into each other's eyes in order to make the unspoken subject clear, and Nicholas Brooke points out that the great eighteenth-century actress Sarah Siddons took a pause at the end of the short line, "O never / Shall sun that morrow see" to do so.[19] This is an important juncture in the play and Lady Macbeth now switches her mode of address to the formal *you* as she implies that serious business is at hand. She pushes her husband because she knows that becoming king is what he desires. Macbeth, however, despite his seeming resolution at the end of the previous scene, does not commit himself, saying only, "We will speak further."[20]

Tomorrow

In the great soliloquy that follows Macbeth's exit from the offstage banquet for Duncan, Macbeth's internal debate reaches its poetic height. It is replete with rhetorical figures and antithetical statements – and is stunning, if somewhat choppy verse. It is choppy because Macbeth is in a state of turmoil. Shakespeare conveys this by putting Macbeth's thoughts in phrases of constantly varying lengths in these verse lines:

> If it were done when 'tis done, then 'twere well
> It were done quickly; if th' assassination
> Could trammel up the consequence and catch
> With his [Duncan's] surcease, success, that but this blow
> Might be the be-all and the end-all – here,
> But here, upon this bank and shoal of time,
> We'd jump the life to come. But in these cases
> We still have judgment here, that we but teach
> Bloody instructions, which being taught, return
> To plague th'inventor. This even-handed justice
> Commends th'ingredience of our poisoned chalice
> To our own lips . . .
> And pity, like a naked new-born babe,
> Striding the blast, or Heaven's cherubim, horsed
> Upon the sightless couriers of the air,
> Shall blow the horrid deed in every eye
> That tears shall drown the wind.[21]

Once again, Macbeth retreats from moving forward with murder. Hamlet is the unexpected analog here. The warrior and the philosopher have this in common: too many words get in the way of action. In *Hamlet*, events inevitably force action. In *Macbeth*, words fail to prevent action. Tomorrow comes either way.

Macbeth asks questions and poses conundrums because he has an imagination that allows him to see the consequences of actions. He literally has visions and begins to see "what another would merely *think*."[22] McAnuff pointed out in rehearsal how his visions take more and more concrete shape as the play progresses. In this soliloquy, he visualizes the abstract concept of pity as a "naked new-born babe." In his next soliloquy at the top of Act Two, he will actually reach out to grasp the dagger that he visualizes before him, but that we do not see. In the banquet scene, he will actually see the Ghost of the murdered Banquo, and the audience shares that vision as well. Shakespeare moves beyond dialogue to force us to experience the nightmare literally through his eyes.

Lady Macbeth, by contrast, is a woman of action: she begins the play with the confidence of a practical person who sees the direct route. Her language is equally direct, if *usually* more pedestrian than her husband's. In general her meter is more regular than his and she uses fewer metaphors. She rarely speaks in extended imagery or extends her thoughts beyond the present: she has little appreciation of consequences and so later is shattered by them.

In 1.7, when she is angry with her husband for leaving the offstage banquet, she uses the formal *you* to address him: "Was the hope drunk / Wherein you dressed yourself?"[23] She then switches to the intimate *thou* when she wants to be seductive: "From this time, / Such I account thy love. Art thou afeard / To be the same in thine own act and valour / As thou art in desire?"[24] She will continue to go back and forth between these modes in this scene and the change in pronoun will point the way.

Macbeth brings up the question of what makes a man, a fundamental and ongoing question in this play: "I dare do all that may become a man, / Who dares do more is none."[25] She counters by attacking his manhood and boldly bringing up the subject of children, an important motif in the play. Her famous line about dashing out her "babe's" brains[26] is so startling that it almost eclipses two significant details. She admits that she loved that babe, and she understands that the subject of children is the knockout punch that she can throw at him.

Macbeth contains an unusual number of sons among its cast of characters, and with the exception of Donalbain, Macbeth kills or tries to kill them all. His attempt to kill Fleance is a failure, but he gets better at it, ordering the successful murder of Macduff's children and killing Seyward's son himself in combat at the end of the play. Babes are also memorable images in the play, from the "naked new-born babe" cited in his soliloquy above who would "blow the deed in every eye" to the children who are apparitions in the cauldron scene. Cleanth Brooks describes Macbeth's "war on children" as a war on "the future Macbeth would control and cannot control."[27] Time and its variants will become one of the most frequently used words in the play.[28] The Macbeths are a childless couple who put their energy into his career. That is how she expresses her love for him.

Macbeth replies to her challenge on children with a question (quoting the Folio version):

Macbeth If we should faile?
Lady M We faile?
But screw your courage to the sticking place,
And wee'l not fayle . . .[29]

At this time printers also used a question mark to indicate an exclamation point. Should the second question mark above be an exclamation point? The difference is critical. A question mark indicates that Lady Macbeth does not believe they will fail. An exclamation point would indicate that if they fail, so be it: at least they have tried. Brooke's edition notes that Sarah Siddons used the question mark in productions early in her career and then changed her reading of the lines to an exclamation point.[30]

Lady Macbeth finally engages her husband by getting him to participate in the planning of Duncan's demise with these words:

> . . . Will it not be received
> When *we* have marked with blood those sleepy two [grooms]
> Of his own chamber, and used their very daggers,
> That they have done't? . . .
> Away, and mock the time with fairest show,
> False face must hide what the false heart doth know.[31]

Notice how cleverly Shakespeare inserts the motif of time into the mix. Time, as we will see, will eventually mock them.

These are the points of departure for the Macbeths. They begin the play in different places. However you define them at the top you must account for their divergent journey, a chief characteristic of this play. Macbeth's regime falls apart, but why does Lady Macbeth fall apart in a way that Macbeth does not? These are questions we will explore as we continue to excavate the play.

And tomorrow

At the top of Act Two Macbeth steps up from masking and equivocation to an outright lie. Banquo refers to the Sisters when he says, "To you they have shown some truth." Shakespeare has Macbeth complete the verse line, perhaps to indicate his response is too automatic to be an honest denial, perhaps to hide the lie in a short response: "I think not of them."[32]

In the soliloquy that follows this scene, Macbeth's ability to anticipate the consequences of his actions produces the vision of the dagger. Once again his ability to see ahead stops him in his tracks and he reverts to a reverie of words. Macbeth compares his approach to Duncan's chamber to Prince Tarquin's to another bedroom, that of the Roman matron in Shakespeare's poem *The Rape of Lucrece*. Historically, her disgrace by a member of the royal house brought down the Roman monarchy and paved the way for an elected republic. Macbeth's tyranny will also bring about the establishment of a new kind of regime in Scotland.

Macbeth's reverie on the dagger ends with a major turning point in the play: "Whiles I threat, he lives; / Words to the heat of deeds too cold breath gives."[33] A bell rings to punctuate this decision. It is the signal from Lady Macbeth that all is clear, but he has already decided to move forward with the murder without her prompting.

Why does Macbeth finally reject his interior debates? Scholars offer differing answers. The most persuasive for me comes from Stephen Greenblatt in *Will in the World*. He argues that by the time of his great tragedies Shakespeare *chose* not to provide clear answers to questions of motivation:

> Shakespeare's work had long been wryly skeptical of official explanations and excuses – the accounts, whether psychological or theological, of why people behave the way they do. . . . With *Hamlet*, Shakespeare found that if he refused to provide himself or his audience with a familiar comforting rationale that seems to make it all make sense, he could get to something immeasurably deeper.[34]

Shakespeare shed the fallacy that life can be boxed in a comfortable package. This is what later adaptations of his plays tried to do. This is what some scholars try to do. This too was my struggle in writing this book: the seduction of neat summaries. Shakespeare resists reductive intellectualization. He is an artist: he expands our thinking by allowing us to decide. I will continue to explore the implications of that extraordinary aspect of his writing in subsequent chapters and how what Greenblatt calls Shakespeare's "strategic opacity"[35] opens up our access to his plays.

We experience the extraordinary scene that follows entirely through the overwrought emotions of our two murderers. It is dark, and sounds are used to stunning effect to reveal another side of Lady Macbeth. An owl startles her as she waits for her husband to commit the murder. She hears her husband's voice offstage and nearly falls apart: "Alack, I am afraid they [Duncan's grooms] have awaked." She follows this with a line that seems uncharacteristic for her: "Had he not resembled / My father as he slept, I had done't [murdered him]."[36] All this seems odd coming from someone composed of steel. Perhaps she is not as unaffected as we think.

Macbeth returns from Duncan's chamber and she calls him "My husband?"[37] for the only time in the play. There is a choice to be made here. Kenneth Muir's Arden edition changes the Folio's question mark to an exclamation point to show that she can see his bloody hands and emphasize that she approves. Brooke keeps the question mark and allows Macbeth's response to answer her question: "I have done the deed."[38]

Macbeth describes the murder scene. Quotation marks are rare or nonexistent in the original texts, and so modern editors have a choice as to where the quote begins and ends in these lines from the Folio version of *Macbeth*:

> Me thought I heard a voyce cry, Sleep [sic] no more:
> *Macbeth* does murther Sleepe, the innocent Sleepe,
> Sleepe that knits vp the rauel'd Sleeve of Care,
> The death of each dayes Life, sore Labor's Bath,
> Balme of hurt Mindes, great Nature's second Course,
> Chiefe nourisher in Life's Feast.[39]

In the Oxford and in Muir's Arden edition the voice begins its cry with "Sleep no more . . ." They differ, however, on where the quote ends. Muir ends the quote after "Macbeth does murder sleep." The Oxford places the close quotation mark at the end of the entire passage.[40]

Macbeth is so distraught that he has brought the daggers he used to murder the King with him. While she returns them to the murder scene, he delivers one of the poetic heights of the play. At this time, the English were still catching up to the Renaissance and their language was being enlarged by the addition of polysyllabic Latinate words from the continent to the old English vocabulary of simple, stolid words. Shakespeare cleverly uses both to great effect in the last two lines, turning an adjective into a verb:

> What hands are here? Ha, they pluck out mine eyes.
> Will all great Neptune's ocean wash this blood
> Clean from my hand? No – this my hand will rather
> The multitudinous seas incarnadine,
> Making the green one red.[41]

Latinate words that arrived with the Renaissance were useful in filling out the syllables of blank verse as seen in line four, but note to what effective use Shakespeare puts the short English words in the final line. Their simplicity punctuates the end of this speech with force, and the short line offers the possibility for a dramatic pause at its conclusion. The image that this line contains repeats what he says in the line above to underline their importance to the play. Macbeth's actions do incarnadine Scotland, which hereafter is described as ill.

When Lady Macbeth returns from Duncan's chamber, she counters Macbeth's powerful poetry with a typically direct eight-word line: "A little water clears us of this deed."[42] Nothing in the play better differentiates their characters than these contrasting lines. This water imagery culminates with that of Lady Macbeth in her sleepwalking scene, where we powerfully witness the fallacy of her statement here. The forward-looking Macbeth, however, has this realization now.

Earlier, Macbeth expressed the desire that "the eye wink at the hand."[43] Now Macbeth concludes this scene with another realization: "To know my deed, 'twere best not know myself."[44] These are further steps in what Nicholas Brooke calls Macbeth's "self-division."[45]

Suddenly, at a time when the Macbeths are at their most fragile, there is a knocking at the door. They retreat from the stage, but Macduff continues to knock. Shakespeare gives him prominence by introducing him late in the play. He is waiting impatiently to say his first lines, but first the Porter enters to offer a few words of his own.

Notes

1 Anthony Brennan, *Shakespeare's Dramatic Structures* (Routledge, 1986), p. 119.
2 *Macbeth*, ed. Nicholas Brooke (Oxford World Classics, 1994), 1.4.52.
3 Ibid., 1.3.51–52.
4 Ibid., 1.3.70.
5 Ibid., 1.3.128–30
6 Ibid., 1.3.140.
7 Ibid., 1.3.144–45.
8 Ibid., 1.3.150–53.
9 Ibid., 2.1.58.
10 Ibid., 1.4.14–30.
11 Ibid., 1.4.49–54.
12 The Norton Facsimile: *The First Folio of Shakespeare*, ed. Charlton Hinman (W. W. Norton, 1968), p. 742.
13 *Macbeth*, ed. Nicholas Brooke (Oxford World Classics, 1994), 1.5.56–57.
14 Ibid., 1.5.10. For the further use of thou and you between husband and wife, see p. 148.
15 Ibid., 1.5.40 and 1.5.50–51.
16 Ibid., 1.5.57; 3.2.32, 39 and 48.
17 Ibid., 1.5.53 and 61; 3.4.130.
18 Stephen Greenblatt, *Will in the World* (Norton, 2004), p. 137.
19 *Macbeth*, ed. Nicholas Brooke (Oxford World Classics, 1994), note on line 1.5.59–60. Siddons was considered the great eighteenth-century tragedienne.
20 Ibid., 1.5.69.

21 Ibid., 1.7.1–25.
22 *Macbeth*, ed. George Lyman Kittredge (Ginn and Co., 1939), p. XIV.
23 *Macbeth*, ed. Nicholas Brooke (Oxford World Classics, 1994), 1.7.35–36.
24 Ibid., 1.7.38–41.
25 Ibid., 1.7.46–47.
26 Ibid., 1.7.55.
27 Cleanth Brooks, "The Naked Babe and the Cloak of Manliness," in *The Well Wrought Urn* (Harcourt Brace, 1947), p. 45. Brooks shows how imagery can lead us to the heart of the play.
28 Concordances to Shakespeare's work count the number of times a word is used in a given play.
29 The Norton Facsimile: *The First Folio of Shakespeare*, ed. Charlton Hinman (Norton, 1968), 1.7.539–42.
30 *Macbeth*, ed. Nicholas Brooke (Oxford World's Classics, 1994), note to 1.7.60–61.
31 Ibid., 1.7.75–83.
32 Ibid., 2.1.22.
33 Ibid., 2.1.61–62.
34 Greenblatt, *Will in the World*, p. 324.
35 Ibid., p. 324.
36 *Macbeth*, ed. Nicholas Brooke (Oxford World Classics, 1994), 2.2.10–14.
37 Ibid., 2.2.14.
38 Ibid., 2.2.14–15.
39 The Norton Facsimile, ed. Hinman, 2.2.691–96.
40 *Macbeth*, ed. Nicholas Brooke (Oxford World Classics), 2.2.34–39; *Macbeth*, ed. Muir, Arden Second Series (Methuen, 1951), 2.2.34–35.
41 *Macbeth*, ed. Nicholas Brooke (Oxford World Classics, 1994), 2.2.58–62.
42 Ibid., 2.2.66.
43 Ibid., 1.4.53.
44 Ibid., 2.2.72.
45 Ibid., note on 2.2.72.

Bibliography

Shakespeare editions cited

Macbeth. Ed. Nicholas Brooke. Oxford World's Classics, 1994.
Macbeth. Ed. George Lyman Kittredge. Gin and Co., 1939.
Macbeth. Ed. Kenneth Muir, Arden Second Series. Methuen, 1951.
The Norton Facsimile: *The First Folio of Shakespeare*. Ed. Charlton Hinton. Norton, 1968.

Other sources

Brennan, Anthony. *Shakespeare's Dramatic Structures*. Routledge, 1986.
Brooks, Cleanth. *The Well-Wrought Urn*. Harcourt Brace, 1947.
Greenblatt, Stephen. *Will in the World*. Norton, 2004.

10 Remember the Porter

Today, the Porter scene is celebrated for the audacious way in which Shakespeare brings comedy into the play as a welcome emotional release for the audience after the murder of Duncan. For a hundred years, however, this scene was cut from *Macbeth* because it was considered vulgar and an aesthetic atrocity. As with other odd scenes that are dismissed solely as comic interludes, however, the scene provides a perspective that is essential to understanding Shakespeare's play.

The Porter is a riff on a character that Shakespeare probably saw as a child. In biblical apocrypha, Christ "descended into hell" after his crucifixion in order to release souls who were sent there for venial sins. In the Harrowing of Hell episode of the medieval mystery play cycles, Christ encounters a comic porter there. Shakespeare's Porter refers to him: "if a man were porter of Hell Gate, he should have old turning the key."[1] Shakespeare gives him working-class vernacular: the porter of hell will get old turning the key because so many people are sent there. Just how many there are we shall soon see, as the inebriated Porter welcomes a series of sinners into the hell that the Macbeths' castle has become.

In the next line, the Porter delivers the first recorded "Knock, knock" joke in print, as Macduff knocks on the door. "Who's there?" the Porter asks, as he describes three sinners for our entertainment.[2] The first is a farmer who hanged himself after the grain he hoarded to drive up its price instead lost its value. Next the Porter welcomes an equivocator, someone who (as previously mentioned) lies by playing with the meaning of words. The third sinner is a tailor who skimps on the cloth needed for an order to maximize his profit. Moisés Kaufman for his 2006 production in New York's Central Park wanted the audience to hear this celebrated scene in a fresh way. He cast Lynn Cohen, a maid, as the Porter, for the production's World War I setting. I suggested that we update the list of sinners. The greedy farmer, the equivocator, and the thieving tailor were the butt of jokes in Shakespeare's time, but obscure in ours. We decided that, if Shakespeare used English references specific to his time for a play set in eleventh-century Scotland, we could update the Porter's sinners to *our* present. Also, the monologue at times has a tone that sets it apart, approaching that of standup comedy. We felt this gave us permission to try to restore just how startling this scene, coming after Duncan's murder, may have been for its original audience.

The limitation we gave ourselves was to change as few words as possible. This was easy to do in the case of the first two sinners, where we only changed two words. Minimal changes in the language used to describe the third sinner proved more difficult, but we were able to retain the sin of stealing and the sexual overtones. The ten words we substituted are italicized in our emendation below. To focus on the changes to the sinners, I have elided other lines in this passage that we retained in our production:

> Here's a *merchant*, that hanged himself on th'expectation of plenty . . . Faith, here's a *legislator*, that could swear in both the scales against either scale, who committed treason enough for God's sake, yet could not equivocate to heaven . . . Faith, here's a *priest*, come hither, for stealing *the innocence of a young boy*. Come in, *priest*, here you may roast your goose.[3]

The change from farmer to merchant drew little reaction from the audience. Few probably noticed it, but the idea of the line was clearer and the audience did not drop out because they were confused. Confusion is deadly in live theatre, where any time spent trying to understand what was just said prevents the audience from listening to the next lines. The change from equivocator to legislator, however, drew approving laughter, and we retained the word *equivocate* to set up its continued usage both in this scene and later, as well as for its importance to the play. Our boldest change, however, provided the greatest reaction. The audience roared in approval when they heard the topical line about the priest.

This rethinking of the Porter scene had its roots in a previous production I had worked on at La Jolla. Des McAnuff had his Porter, Jefferson Mays, talk directly to the audience using Shakespeare's language.[4] This entirely changed the dynamic of this section of the scene, as it set up a relationship between the Porter and the audience. We built on this idea in Moisés' production. When Lynn talked about the merchant, she found one in the audience. When she talked about the legislator, she found someone who could be one. The unlucky person who was chosen for the priest laughed along with the rest of the audience. Moisés made it clear that Lynn was talking to specific members of the audience by shining a spotlight on them in our outdoor theatre. In a subsequent production at the indoor theatre of the Stratford Shakespeare Festival (2008), McAnuff had his Porter, Tom

Rooney, use a flashlight to find his updated sinners in the audience. All this enlivened the opening section of the scene and proved that the best way to be true to Shakespeare is to rise to his level of audacity.

"What are you?"

After the Porter welcomes the three sinners, Macduff knocks again and the Porter responds:

> Knock, knock. Never at quiet – what are you? – But this place is too cold for Hell. I'll devil-porter it no further: I had thought to have let in some of all professions, that go the primrose way to th'everlasting bonfire.[5]

The Oxford editor, Nicholas Brooke, added the dashes, which usually indicate an interruption in thought or the person addressed. Here, that choice seems to indicate that the Porter abruptly ends his riff to speak for the first time to the actual person knocking off stage. In this configuration, "What are you?" means "Who's at the door?" This is the usual explanation of a line that has puzzled scholars and long eluded me as well. The dashes however, are not in the Folio: they are editorial. If they are removed and the transition is not abrupt, then to whom is "What are you?" addressed?

I have come to believe that "What are you?" is a continuation of the Porter's direct address. If he continues to welcome members of the audience into hell, "What are you?" becomes a challenge to us: what kind of sinner are you? The lines that follow then become specific rather than generic. The Porter says, "But, this place is too cold for hell," because of the number of sinners in the audience. "I had thought to have let in some of all the professions, that go the primrose way to th'everlasting bonfire," refers to number of professions he finds in the audience. With this choice, the Porter's scene becomes more than a comic diversion. It becomes essential to Shakespeare's play.

Shakespeare's plays are only fully revealed when we put them on their feet in three dimensions, as he intended, in rehearsal and eventually in performance. The audience is the partner for the actor who plays the Porter at the top of his scene, and the meaning of these lines, however you choose to interpret them, can only be fully understood in its presence. "What are you?" is a critical part of the discourse in *Macbeth*. It is the question that Macbeth asks the Sisters in his first scene in the play, and here Shakespeare asks it of us as well. As the Macbeths' crimes multiply and become more heinous, Shakespeare will continue to detach us from them in the second half of the play. But here, just after the first murders, Shakespeare in the guise of the Porter looks us in the eye and reminds us that we all are sinners. That is the function of this section of the Porter scene and the reason why he goes on at such length about sinners.

At the end of *Romeo and Juliet*, the Prince tells us that "All are punished,"[6] and all are indeed implicated in that tragedy, even the young lovers. By the time Shakespeare wrote *Macbeth*, he extends his remarkable, even-handed point of view to his audience as well. The Porter asks that we "remember" him at the end of this section to solicit a tip *and* to remind us to heed what he has said. In the Porter scene, Shakespeare had so mastered the craft of playwriting that he uses mode of address to convey content and those three words – "What are you?" – to implicate us in his play. This was a technique he was already exploring in his development of the soliloquy.

Shakespeare and Hitchcock

The Macbeths dominate the first two acts. They are in all but three scenes, and the longest of these focuses on Macbeth's prowess on the battlefield. We experience much of this part of the play through the eyes of Shakespeare's murderers. Alfred Hitchcock uses the same technique in films such as *Strangers on a Train*, *Vertigo*, and *Psycho*. They are so disturbing in part because he makes us identify with his murderers. That seemingly most gentle of playwrights, Thornton Wilder, writes about identification in theatre in a seminal essay in a preface to an edition of his plays. It includes these words: "We have all murdered, in thought; and been murdered."[7]

Earlier in his career, Shakespeare made us complicit with another murderer, Richard III, at least at the beginning of that play, by having him *share* his thoughts in direct address to us. In delivering his soliloquies Richard must address the audience. He is seducing us. That is his *modus operandi* with everyone, including the audience. A choice must always be made with Shakespeare's soliloquies: does the character address the audience or not? That choice is critical both to how we perceive Shakespeare's characters and how we understand the individual plays. The great Shakespearean director Michael Langham suggests this:

> If you are talking *to* an audience with "To be or not to be," you really aren't inside that speech. I think it's too deeply personal and introspectively irrational a speech for direct address. But . . . with Edmund in *Lear* or Iago in *Othello* or Richard III, Shakespeare's hint . . . seems to be, "Go on, make the audience into your accomplice."[8]

Langham's remarks can help us to understand how Shakespeare intends us to perceive the character of Macbeth. He is not conceived in the mode of Shakespeare's great *villains*: Richard, Edmund, or Iago. They share their thoughts with us in direct address in order to seduce us, at least temporarily, and Shakespeare detaches us from them well before the end. That is similar to Hitchcock's method in *Strangers on a Train*. Macbeth, however, is conceived in the mode of Shakespeare's flawed tragic figures – Hamlet, Othello, and Lear. We overhear their most personal thoughts. In this way Shakespeare creates a bond between these characters and the audience, but it is Shakespeare who is seducing us so that we retain sympathy for them, if in varying degrees, to the end. Hitchcock does this as well with his murderers in his masterworks, *Vertigo* and *Psycho*, where Norman Bates reminds us that "We all go a little crazy at times."[9] And it is this approach that makes *Macbeth*, with its presentation of the darkest of Shakespeare's tragic figures, one of his most disturbing and modern plays.

Notes

1 *Macbeth*, ed. Nicholas Brooke (Oxford World Classics, 1994), 2.3.1–2.
2 Ibid., 2.3.3.
3 Ibid., 2.3.4–14, with word substitutions in italics.
4 Des McAnuff's production at the La Jolla Playhouse in 1989.
5 *Macbeth*, ed. Nicholas Brooke (Oxford World Classics), 2.3.15–18.
6 *Romeo and Juliet*, ed. Jill L. Levenson (Oxford World's Classics, 2000), 5.3.295
7 Thornton Wilder, Preface in *Three Plays* (Harper Perennial Modern Classics, 2006), p. xxvi.
8 Michael Langham, "The Lightness of Shakespeare," *The Journal for Stage Directors & Choreographers* 14, no. 1 (Spring/Summer 2000), p. 12.
9 Alfred Hitchcock, director, and Joseph Stephano, screenwriter. *Psycho* (Paramount Pictures, 1960).

Bibliography

Shakespeare editions cited

Macbeth. Ed. Nicholas Brooke. Oxford World Classics, 1994.

The Norton Facsimile: *The First Folio of Shakespeare*. Ed. Charlton Hinman. Norton, 1968.

Romeo and Juliet. Ed. Jill L. Levenson. Oxford World's Classics, 2000.

Other sources

Coleridge, Samuel Taylor. "Lectures 1808–1819 on Literature II." In *The Collected Works*, ed. R. A. Foakes, vol. 5. Princeton, NJ, 1987.

Alfred Hitchcock, director, and Joseph Stephano, screenplay. *Psycho*. Paramount Pictures, 1960.

Langham, Michael. "The Lightness of Shakespeare." *The Journal for Stage Directors & Choreographers* 14, no. 1 (Spring/Summer 2000), pp. 9–13.

Wilder, Thornton. *Three Plays by Wilder*. Harper Collins, 1957.

11 The public story

Knowledge that can help us understand plays comes in many forms. Chekhov's journals are immensely helpful in understanding that writer's work. He writes about his beliefs about the world, his life, his plays, and his reactions to his productions. We can find a context for their writing in biographies about him. With Shakespeare, documentary information on his life is extremely limited. We must even use conjecture to posit the exact order in which his plays were written.

Bill Bryson's biography of Shakespeare sticks close to the facts and avoids speculation: "Before he settled in London and became celebrated as a playwright, history provides just four recorded glimpses of Shakespeare – at his baptism [April 26, 1564], his wedding [November 1582], and the . . . births of his [three] children."[1] The two who survived to adulthood were Judith and Susanna, which may account for the continued presence of so many daughters in his plays. Stephen Greenblatt's biography is brimming with pertinent descriptions of the period in which Shakespeare lived.[2] Greenblatt writes about the flourishing playwriting scene that Shakespeare encountered in London and an England that was moving from a medieval to a modern world, a regular preoccupation in Shakespeare's plays and important to the two at the center of this book.

If we know only the outlines of Shakespeare's life, however, his plays reveal his preoccupations, and *analogs* from them can help us understand individual plays. Leadership and succession were important in the latter days of the childless Elizabeth's reign, and Shakespeare's examination of the mechanisms of power and what makes an effective leader in his English history plays continued with the monarchs of many of his tragedies. In *Henry IV*, it is the honorable Hotspur who dies. He will not become king, nor will the honorable Macduff. The cool-headed Malcolm and Prince Hal will. The future Henry V is capable of using people, as he declares in an early monologue in *I Henry IV*,[3] and Malcolm is kin to him. Both are willing to affect loose behavior to achieve their ends, as we will see with Malcolm in Act Four.

In *The Weak King Dilemma*, Michael Manheim discusses the impact of the "pirated translations" of Machiavelli's *The Prince* that began to appear in England in the 1570s, decades after that book appeared on the continent.[4] *The Prince* was still a hot topic of discussion when the character of Hal first took the stage in *Henry IV* in the 1590s. Gary Taylor points out that in *Henry V* there is actually a paraphrase of one of the key questions raised in *The Prince*: is it better for a leader to be feared or loved? Henry V, we are told, is both "feared and loved."[5] This informed our investigation of Malcolm at La Jolla Playhouse and at Stratford. It is important to remember, however, that analogs trace *patterns*. Malcolm, Hal, and their brethren in two other plays – Fortinbras and Edgar – will probably be better kings than their predecessors, but they are not the same characters.

Three kings

Analogs compare similarities in different plays. Contrasts between characters in the same play are particularly important in drama because conflict is usually built around them. In *Macbeth*, Shakespeare records an evolution from a feudal society in which a king must contend with powerful chieftains, to a warrior-king who fights on the battlefield, to a powerful king who strategizes and organizes, but does not fight in battle. This is congruent with information that Shakespeare discovered in his source material.

At the beginning of *Macbeth*, we witness the power of Duncan's chieftains. Scotland is in chaos and Duncan's kingdom faces two simultaneous military threats. Both involve fellow Scots. The "rebel" Macdonald challenges Duncan with revolt from within the kingdom; Cawdor is the "traitor" who assists an invasion from abroad by the King of Norway.[6]

Historical reading provides us with a context for Duncan's comment about Cawdor: he was "a gentleman on whom I built / An absolute trust."[7] Raphael Holinshed in his *History of Scotland* describes Duncan this way:

> After it was perceiued how negligent [Duncan] was in punishing offendors, manie misruled persons tooke occasion thereof to trouble the peace and quiet state of the common-wealth, by seditious commotions.[8]

What do the characters in *Macbeth* say about him? He may be "gracious Duncan,"[9] as both Macbeth and Lenox call him, but is he an effective king? In their long scene in Act Four, Macduff seems to confirm his goodness when he tells Malcolm that "Thy royal father / Was a most sainted king."[10] Macduff uses religious allusions earlier when he discovers Duncan's body.

In fact much of the praise that we hear for Duncan comes out of the mouth of Macduff. Shakespeare frequently quotes or paraphrases passages from the Bible in his plays, but his characters usually do not use its language consciously. Macduff does, and that tells us something about *him*: he is a religious man with traditional views on the crown. Shakespeare is not sentimental, however, and goodness and good leadership may not go hand in hand. Viewed through the lens of Shakespeare's history plays, Duncan is one of Shakespeare's weak kings and, as with Richard II and Henry VI, is killed by (or on behalf of) his successor.

Duncan does understand the political threat a war hero such as Macbeth poses to his standing. When they first meet in the play, he is careful to lavish praise on Macbeth in front of his assembled court in the passage quoted earlier. His decision to visit the Macbeths at their castle may have been recognized by Elizabethans as a political tactic as well. Under the guise of conveying an honor, a "royal progress" was a way for the monarch to assert his or her authority by forcing a sometimes tricky subject to entertain the king or queen and their entourage at the subject's expense. Elizabeth I regularly used it to her advantage. Duncan's "gracious" dialogue with Lady Macbeth on his arrival at her castle is the most convoluted in the play. We know she is being insincere; he gilds his language as well. Duncan is smart enough to question why Macbeth is not there to greet him when he enters his castle. He may not be a warrior king, as is Macbeth, or an effective leader, as his son will become, but he is not stupid.

Macbeth is presented as a great warrior, right from the beginning. Scotland is only saved because of his and Banquo's military capabilities. Even before he enters the play, there is an extraordinary description in 1.2 of Macbeth as Arnold Schwarzenegger on the battlefield, as he corners the rebel, Macdonald:

> For brave Macbeth – well he deserves that name –
> Disdaining Fortune, with his brandished steel
> Which smoked with bloody execution,
> Like Valour's minion carved out his passage
> Till he faced the slave –
> [And] ne'er shook hands nor bade farewell to him,
> Till he unseamed him from the nave to th' chops,
> And fixed his head upon our battlements.[11]

Macbeth's ability to anticipate may have served him well as a military leader, but his ability to see consequences will later thwart his tenure as king. In Shakespeare's play, he becomes so preoccupied with maintaining his position that he is constantly reactive. His growing paranoia leads to further murders, which alienate both his court and his country. We do not know what kind of king Macbeth would have made had he not murdered Duncan, but the word most frequently used to describe him after he becomes king is "tyrant." It is used fifteen times in the second half of the play, three times more than in any other play by Shakespeare. The *OED* defines *tyrant* both as "one who seizes upon the sovereign power . . . without legal right; an absolute ruler" and "a king or ruler who exercises his power in an oppressive, unjust, or cruel manner; a despot."[12] Macbeth becomes all of these. Being called a tyrant was the most damning term that could be thrown at a king by the English, who began to limit the power of the monarch as early as 1215 in the Magna Carta.

What the third king in this trio – Malcolm – represents will be examined later in this chapter.

A trio of Thanes

The public story of *Macbeth* also includes a parade of Thanes, and the critical trio among them are defined by their contrasting actions. At the end of Act Two, in the first of the three choral scenes that ends each of the play's middle acts, the Thane of Ross gets a surprising answer from the Thane of Fife (italics added):

ROSS . . . Will you to Scone [for the coronation]?
MACDUFF
No, cousin; I'll [home] to Fife.
ROSS *Well*, I will thither [to Scone].
MACDUFF
Well, may you see things *well* done there: – adieu,
Lest our old robes sit easier than our new.[13]

Shakespeare's ability to say so much with a few words is an example of the extraordinary compression in this play. Macduff tells Ross that he will not attend Macbeth's coronation: he has become suspicious of Macbeth in the public gathering that follows Duncan's murder. Ross' use of *well* covers his surprise at Macduff's decision. He is savvy enough not to ask why. An atmosphere of fear has overtaken Scotland after the assassination of the King, and some things must remain unspoken. Ross's choice to go to the coronation prompts Macduff's sarcastic double repetition of "well." This point will be clear, if all three *wells* are the emphasized syllable in their respective feet, making the first two trochees.

Some scholars see Ross as a shady figure, but I think that is a judgment of a kind that Shakespeare does not make. He simply presents us, with no apologies, with someone who is all too familiar – a figure we would recognize in government or in business today. Ross is savvy enough to accommodate, at least temporarily, whoever has the favor or the power. In Act One, when he delivers the message that Duncan has named Macbeth the Thane of Cawdor, Ross is so full of praise for Macbeth that Angus comments on it. Ross also knows how to be noncommittal, as he is with Macduff here. Later, Ross is rehabilitated when at great risk to himself, he warns Lady Macduff of her peril. This action gives him growth in a play where rehabilitation is an important motif.

Banquo is also part of this pattern. When he and Macbeth first hear the predictions of the Sisters at the top of the play, Banquo gives his "noble partner"[14] good advice: "Oftentimes, to win us to our harm, / The instruments of darkness tell us truths . . . to betray's / In deepest consequence."[15] Note that this is a form of equivocation.

At the top of Act Two, Banquo's integrity is confirmed when he evades Macbeth's overture: "If you shall cleave to my consent, when 'tis, / It shall make honour for you." "So I loose none / In seeking to augment it," is Banquo's careful reply.[16] Later, to the insensitivity of Lady Macbeth's feigned response to Duncan's death – "What, in our house?" – Banquo delivers an admonition: "Too cruel, anywhere."[17] At the end of that scene, after Macbeth begins to fall apart, it is Banquo who takes the lead and suggests that the thanes reassemble later.

It should come as a surprise then, when in his soliloquy at the top of Act Three, Banquo says he will keep his suspicions to himself. The Sisters told him he will become the father of kings, and he soon pays dearly for his choice.[18] Macbeth's noble partner becomes his fourth victim. In the public story of *Macbeth*, both Banquo and Ross compromise themselves under Macbeth's corrupt regime, but there is a significant difference. It is the honorable thane who falls prey to his own ambitions; the questionable thane is rehabilitated. This gives both a journey – and not the ones that we would expect. Actions speak louder than words in this play, an important motif that also applies to Macbeth and his wife. Their journeys too are not anticipated by the words we hear from them in the first half of the play.

In Act Four, Shakespeare continues this pattern as we audit half of that act through a fourth thane, Macduff. The uncertainty and fear that murder has engendered now poisons the entire country, and Scotland in the imagery of the play is now presented as ill. That is why *two* doctors will appear in the play, as Macduff goes to England to find the remedy in Malcolm. How will the righteous thane fare there? Shakespeare frames that question with the *actions* of Banquo and Ross.

Malcolm and Macduff

It is Malcolm who is given the longest scene in the play in his great collision with Macduff in Act Four. Because of the way they are contrasted there, it is useful to discuss the two of them together. Neither is introduced as a warrior. In his first scene Malcolm has returned to the safety of camp from the battlefield where the Sergeant has saved him from capture. Malcolm does seem to know more about the military campaigns than his father, and Duncan relies on him.

Malcolm has no lines in his next scene after Duncan names him as his successor, and we learn little more about him until his appearance after his father's murder. There, Malcolm's reaction is not emotional, but coolly practical: he simply asks, "By whom?"[19] Malcolm is smart enough to understand the peril he and his brother face from the person in the court who killed their father: "To show an unfelt sorrow is an office / Which the false man does easy."[20] He is a good student and has learned the lesson of Cawdor. His tactic of leaving quietly, however, leads to suspicion falling on the two princes and shows Malcolm to be shortsighted at this point in the play. This gives him a journey to the remarkable and savvy character that we meet again in 4.3.

Macduff first appears as a name in Duncan's entourage as they enter Macbeth's castle in 1.6. He speaks no lines, and his position in the court is ambiguous. We first hear him talk when the Porter welcomes him into Macbeth's castle after Duncan's murder. He tells the Porter he is there to give Duncan his wake-up call: "He did command me to call timely on him. . . . For 'tis my *limited* service [italics added]."[21] Macduff's late entrance sets him apart from the fawning and politics that we see at the court. Like Banquo, he seems to be an honorable man.

Macduff's first lines to the Porter are terse and to the point. He is kind enough to humor the Porter in their exchange on equivocation, until his sense of duty intrudes. After he discovers the murder, his language becomes highly emotional. He repeatedly uses the rhetorical form *epizeuxis*, the repetition of a single word with none intervening: he repeats *horror* three times; *awake*, *up*, and *Banquo*, twice each.[22] He uses extended religious references and refers to Duncan respectfully as "royal master . . . royal father."[23] His traditional attitudes about the king extend to his conservative attitudes about women: "O gentle lady, / 'Tis not for you to hear what I can speak: / The repetition in a woman's ear would murder as it fell."[24] Most important, he is the first thane to challenge Macbeth after hearing the report of Duncan's murder: he asks Macbeth why he killed Duncan's chamberlains.

In summary, Macduff seems to be direct, a bit foursquare, but emotional and volatile, which is important to 4.3, where Malcolm exploits Macduff's reaction to the announcement of the murder of his family. He is a pious and dutiful subject with limited charge. This gives him a point of departure in becoming the warrior-avenger later in the play.

It takes two

In 4.2, Shakespeare brings on a new character, Lady Macduff, for the most horrific scene in the play. We have moved away from the focus on the Macbeths to characters that show us the consequences of the Macbeths' actions. The opening of the scene is entirely about Macduff's limitations as a human being: "Wisdom? To leave his wife, to leave his babes, / . . . He wants the natural touch."[25] Lady Macduff has a right to be angry. Her husband is so consumed by duty that he leaves his family in danger. We may give his lack of foresight various modifiers – naiveté and patriotism are two – but his focus on present needs prevents him from anticipating the likely outcome of his actions. He shares this trait with Lady Macbeth. Later, that singular focus will make him a good avenger. Note that Lady Macduff loves her husband despite her anger. When asked where her husband is, she tells the men who are about to slaughter her family, "I hope in no place so unsanctified / Where such as thou mayst find him."[26]

Shakespeare devotes nearly a tenth of *Macbeth* to the scene that follows, which is perhaps the longest among odd scenes in Shakespeare's plays. Malcolm begins by suggesting to Macduff that they seek shade. This is the first indication that we are moving out of dark interiors, night and nightmare, into the outdoors; it is the first unmurky daylight in the play. Shakespeare confirms this imagery in the scene's concluding line, "The night is long that never finds the day."[27]

Malcolm and Macduff are contrasted from the beginning. Malcolm is wary and his opening words are ambiguous: "Let us . . . Weep our sad bosoms empty." Macduff is typically direct: "Let us rather / Hold fast the mortal sword."[28] Malcolm characterizes himself as "a weak, poor, innocent lamb," but this is a ruse.[29] We learn later that he already has the offer of the English earl, Seyward, and 10,000 men. Malcolm is suspicious of Macduff and challenges him with the obvious question: "Why in that rawness left you wife, and child?" Macduff angrily skirts the question and uses the familiar *thou* in his response to his superior – "Fare thee well, lord, / I would not be the villain that thou think'st."[30] Malcolm, however, stops him with another deception.

The long sequence that follows is difficult to bring off in production. Its dynamics must be understood in order to find the proper cuts and direct the audience to the real action of this section. Malcolm distrusts Macduff's intentions and tests him by lying about his supposed vices. He wants Macduff to reject the man he pretends to be. For his part, Macduff wants Malcolm to lead the Scottish forces against Macbeth and compromises himself for the sake of his country by finding excuses for each of these "vices." In this play, even the righteous thane is compromised. Eventually, Malcolm must threaten that he will "Pour the sweet milk of concord into Hell, / Uproar the universal peace, confound / All unity on earth,"[31] in order to get the angry rejection that will prove Macduff can be trusted.

When he does, Malcolm abandons his gambit and switches from the formal *you* to the friendly, peer-implying *thou* with Macduff. He appeals to Macduff's piety by using phrases such as "devilish," "God above," "at no time broke my faith," "Devil," "miraculous," "holy prayers," and "heavenly gift"[32] – words that were not a previous part of his vocabulary. The atmosphere of distrust, however, is not so easily shaken. Malcolm has lied so expertly about his vices that Macduff is not convinced. "Such welcome and unwelcome things at once / 'Tis hard to reconcile," is his wary reaction.[33] It should influence ours as well. Malcom is one cunning prince: can we really trust him?

Ross now enters and delivers the ammunition Malcolm needs to win over Macduff. Note how key poetic images and motifs help to create one of the most painful passages in the play. The Prince and the Thane are again contrasted. Macduff's reaction to the slaughter of his family is a guilty, "And I must be from thence!" Malcolm's reaction is so instantaneous and self-serving it seems cruel, "Be comforted. / Let's make us med'cines of our great revenge, / To cure this deadly grief." Why deadly grief? Because dwelling on grief will not get Malcolm what he needs from Macduff – action. Shakespeare now gives Malcolm the same imagery that Lady Macbeth used to challenge her husband in 1.7: "Dispute it like a man [join the fight]." Macduff, however, has a different interpretation of that word: "I must also feel it as a man [as a human being]." His definition of what is means to be a man is new and a sign of hope in the play. Macduff adds, "Did Heaven look on, / and would not take their part?" This is the agonized culmination of the long line of Macduff's religious imagery, and he calls himself, "Sinful Macduff. / They were all struck for thee." Malcolm coolly seizes the moment: "Be this the whetstone of your sword. Let grief / Convert to anger: Blunt not the heart, enrage it."[34]

Malcolm has become smart, crafty and manipulative, and an expert dissembler. He is a savvy politician for a new age and creates the perfect avenger as he skillfully takes Macduff through grief to action to revenge. "I put myself to thy direction," Malcolm has told Macduff earlier in the scene and he restates it a few lines later, "What I am truly / Is thine, and my poor country's to command."[35] This, however, is not what we see in Act Five, where it is Malcolm who takes the lead in both dialogue and action. It is he, not Macduff, who directs the combined English and Scottish forces. As we have already seen, words and actions frequently contradict each other in the world of this play. This is an area that unites both the public and private stories.

It is the third in this play's trio of kings who is the effective one, and his skillful manipulation of the last of the thanes to enter the play in this scene shows us that. Shakespeare strips away any sentimentality we have about what makes an effective leader in this scene. Malcolm's seduction of Macduff is just as relentless as Lady Macbeth's is of her husband, and placed in a position parallel to the end of the play as her triumph over Macbeth in 1.7 is to the beginning. Malcolm and Macduff have grown through the play. As with the Macbeths, each needs the other to achieve their objectives. The successful pair remains intact; the Macbeths, as we are about to see, will fragment.

In the final speech in the play, Malcolm begins with the royal "we" and rewards his supporters with a new title. He makes the Thanes into Earls, an English title, because he is moving Scotland towards the more stable form of kingdom that existed in England, including lineal succession with a loyalty to king rather than clan.

From Shakespeare's history plays we know he viewed history as cyclical. At the end of *Henry V*, the Chorus tells us that all the land that Henry gained in France during his celebrated reign was lost during that of his son. The tragedy is carried in the public sphere. That is why *Henry V* is a history play. At the end of *Macbeth*, Shakespeare chose not to reveal that the historical Malcolm was eventually forced to submit to English overlords. This would eventually lead to Scotland being absorbed into Great Britain. Shakespeare ends the public story of *Macbeth* at a point of equilibrium. It is the private story that carries the tragedy.

Notes

1 Bill Bryson, *Shakespeare. The World as Stage* (Atlas Books, 2007), p. 43.
2 Stephen Greenblatt, *Will in the World* (Norton, 2004).
3 Prince Hal says of Falstaff and his followers, "I know you all, and will awhile uphold / The unyok'd humour of your idleness . . . So when this loose behavior I throw off . . . My reformation, glitt'ring o'er my fault, / Shall show more goodly." From *Henry IV, Part One*, ed. A. R. Humphreys, Arden Second Series (Methuen, 1960), 1.2.190–209.
4 Michael Manheim, *The Weak King Dilemma* (Syracuse University Press, 1973), p. 11.
5 *Henry V*, ed. Gary Taylor (Oxford World's Classics, 1982), 2.2.25 and the note on it.
6 *Macbeth*, ed. Nicholas Brooke (Oxford World Classics, 2014), 1.2.10 and 52.
7 Ibid., 1.4.13–14.
8 *Macbeth*, ed. Kenneth Muir, Arden Second Series (Methuen, 1951), p. 167. This is a quote from Holinshed's *Chronicles of Scotland*, Shakespeare's chief source for the historical material in the play. Sedition implies threat from within.
9 *Macbeth*, ed. Nicholas Brooke (Oxford World Classics, 2014), 3.1.65 and 3.6.3.
10 Ibid., 4.3.108–9.
11 Ibid., 1.2.16–23.

12 *Oxford English Dictionary* (Oxford University Press, 1971), tyrant: 1 and 3.
13 *Macbeth*, ed. Nicholas Brooke (Oxford World Classics, 2014), 2.4.35–38.
14 Ibid., 1.3.54.
15 Ibid., 1.3.124–27.
16 Ibid., 2.1.26–28.
17 Ibid., 2.3.90.
18 Ibid., 3.1.1–10.
19 Ibid., 2.3.102.
20 Ibid., 2.3.138–39.
21 Ibid., 2.3.44–52.
22 Ibid., 2.3.65, 75, 79, and 88.
23 Ibid., 2.3.89 and 102.
24 Ibid., 2.3.85–88.
25 Ibid., 4.2.6–9.
26 Ibid., 4.2.83–84.
27 Ibid., 4.3.240.
28 Ibid., 4.3.1–3.
29 Ibid., 4.3.16.
30 Ibid., 4.3.26 and 34–35.
31 Ibid., 4.3.98–100.
32 Ibid., 4.3.117, 120, 128–29, 147, 154, and 157.
33 Ibid., 4.3.138–39.
34 Ibid., 4.3.212–28.
35 Ibid., 4.3.122 and 131–32.

Bibliography

Shakespeare editions cited

Henry IV, Part One. Ed. A. R. Humphreys, Arden Second Series. Methuen, 1960.
Henry V. Ed. Gary Taylor. Oxford World's Classics, 1982.
Macbeth. Ed. Kenneth Muir, Arden Second Series. Methuen, 1951.
Macbeth. Ed. Nicholas Brooke. Oxford World Classics, 1994.

Other sources

Bryson, Bill. *Shakespeare: The World as Stage*. Atlas Books, 2007.
Greenblatt, Stephen. *Will in the World*. Norton, 2004.
Manheim, Michael. *The Weak King Dilemma*. Syracuse University Press, 1973.
Oxford English Dictionary. Oxford University Press, 1971.

12 The Shakespeare industry

The conclusion of that private story cannot be properly understood without examining a second time period – that between the writing of the plays and the present. Our view of Shakespeare's plays has been deeply affected by their production history. Malcolm has the last words in Shakespeare's play. A mere fifty years later that distinction was given to Macduff in an adaptation of the play that held the stage for a hundred years. Facelifts of Shakespeare dictated by the aesthetics and biases of subsequent periods have perpetuated false traditions even after they were no longer used. They still influence the way we view his plays today.

The evolution of the performing text

In 1608 the King's Men began performing indoors at the Blackfriars Theatre as well as at the Globe.[1] Shakespeare was already out of fashion by the end of his career. His late plays, the so-called romances – *Pericles, Cymbeline, The Winter's Tale,* and *The Tempest* – were in part a response to a genre being popularized by the writing team of Beaumont and Fletcher, who relied on spectacle that could be more easily achieved in indoor theatres. The addition of Hecate to *Macbeth*, with songs, dances, and flying witches, may have been an early example of "improving" Shakespeare, as Jacobean drama moved closer to opera during the "Andrew Lloyd Webber" phase of its evolution.

In 1642, civil war broke out and the playhouses were closed under the Puritan government. The Globe was demolished in 1644, and Charles I executed in 1649. Eighteen years passed before English theatre took to the stage again with the restoration of Charles's son to the throne, and "Shakespeare and Jonson, the preferred reading of Charles I, returned from exile with Charles II."[2] Theatres turned to older plays to supply their repertory because, after two decades of closure, there was a lack of new plays to feed the repertoire. The stage that they returned to, however, was very different. Theatre had moved indoors, and a shorter thrust stage pushed actors upstage, reducing their intimacy with the audience. William Davenant, the manager of one of the two London companies that received Charles II's royal warrant, introduced changeable scenery to cater to audiences' taste for spectacle. Women replaced boys onstage during the reign of a king who had grown accustomed to seeing women in female roles during his exile in France.

Davenant was an actor and playwright who followed Ben Jonson as poet laureate in 1638. He was the godson of Shakespeare, who used to overnight at the tavern of Davenant's father on trips from London to Stratford, and "liked to believe and let others believe that he was Shakespeare's bastard."[3] Davenant became the prime mover in bringing Shakespeare back to the stage. The Shakespeare that Davenant and other adaptors offered on the Restoration stages, however, increasingly differed from the original texts, even as the Third and Fourth Folios were being printed in this period.

Restoration dramatists and critics found Elizabethan drama distasteful. John Dryden, the Restoration poet and dramatist, wrote, "It is not permissible to set up a character as composed of mighty opposites," in the Preface to his adaptation of *Troilus and Cressida*: "A character . . . is a composition of qualities not contrary to one another."[4] Dryden also collaborated with Davenant on an adaptation of *The Tempest*, which gave Miranda a sister, Ferdinand a rival, and Ariel a lover to conform to the neoclassical aesthetics of balance. They extended the opening shipwreck scene to provide more spectacle and added more songs.

For his 1674 adaptation of *Macbeth*, Davenant gave the Sisters additional songs, scenes, and dances. They exit their first scene flying and fly in at the top of their second, definitely the witches of Elizabethan folklore. The Porter is cut for tonal unity and neoclassical issues of taste, and along with his departure went his contribution in setting up key issues in the play. Minor characters are excised and their lines conflated with others to conform to that age's neoclassical ideals of dramatic unity.

Seyton, for example, absorbs the lines of the Bleeding Captain in 1.2, the Old Man in 2.4, Lenox in 4.1, and the Doctor in 5.1. By doing this, however, Shakespeare's point in introducing Seyton in Act Five is lost: Macbeth must turn to a stranger because his court has abandoned him. Bringing on Seyton earlier diminished the impact of Macbeth's increasing solitude, essential to his journey in Act Five. In addition, the character of Ross is deleted and his lines in 1.2 and 1.4 are given to Macduff, so both Macduff and his wife can be introduced earlier. Cutting Ross is particularly damaging because Shakespeare uses him to show how the act of murder poisons not only the perpetrators, but also those who keep silent.

Davenant's Macduffs are sentimentalized as the good foils for the evil Macbeths in several added scenes. Lady Macduff tells Lady Macbeth about her love for her husband in their duet in Act One; the Macduffs reject the Sisters, whom they meet at the end of Act Two. Davenant brings the Macduffs back again in Act Three, where they discuss ambition, a word Shakespeare uses only three times in *Macbeth*. By comparison, Shakespeare uses ambition/ambitious more often in five plays, including *Hamlet* (nine times), *2 Henry VI* (twelve times) and *Julius Caesar* (fourteen times). Davenant uses ambition six times in the Act Three scene discussed above, where Lady Macduff warns her husband: "Ambition urg'd him to that bloody deed / May you be never by Ambition Led."[5]

In Act Four, Lady Macduff's scene ends before the murderers enter, which softens one of the most brutal scenes in Shakespeare in deference to neoclassical demands for good taste. In doing so, we lose the ugliest illustration of what Macbeth has become. Macduff is the hero of Davenant's play and so it is he, not Malcolm, who has its last words and they are a sermon: "[Macbeth's] vice shall make your [Malcolm's] virtue shine more bright / As a fair day Succeeds a stormy night."[6] Macduff can praise Malcolm's virtues in this way because their long scene in Act Four is drastically cut. Macduff no longer needs to compromise himself by rationalizing away Malcolm's list of supposed vices because those vices take up only four lines in Davenant's adaptation. Macduff's honor remains intact, and Malcolm's questionable tactics are diminished.

As for Davenant's Macbeths, they get a new Act Four scene where she tells her husband that Duncan's ghost has been pursuing her in a speech that sentimentalizes one of the most singular and fascinating characters in Shakespeare:

> . . . the strange error of my eyes [in seeing Duncan's ghost]
> Proceeds from the strange action of your hands
> Distraction did by fitts possess my head
> Because a Crown unjustly covers it
> . . . resign the ill-gaind Crown
> Why shou'd you labour still to be unjust
> There has been too much blood allready spilt
> Make not the Subjects Victims to your guilt.[7]

Nowhere is the damage more deeply felt than in Davenant's reduction of Macbeth's magnificent poetry. Shakespeare gives Macbeth these words, cited earlier from 1.7:

> . . . if th'assassination
> Could trammel up the consequence and catch
> With his [Duncan's] surcease, success, that but this blow

Might be the be-all and the end-all . . .
We'd jump the life to come. But in these cases
We still have judgment here, [so] that we but teach
Bloody instructions, which being taught, return
To plague th'inventor . . .

In Davenant those eight lines become these five:

. . . if his death might be
Without the Death of Nature in my selfe,
And killing my own rest, it wou'd suffice:
But deeds of this Complexion still returne
To plague the doer; and destroy his peace . . .[8]

Davenant falls into the usual trap of those, including me, who change Shakespeare's words in order to make them clearer. Take away the high poetry that Macbeth uses to express his intense, internal struggle, and you lose Shakespeare's conception of an exceptional character who falls from grace. Not only is the poetry flattened, but Shakespeare's play is as well. Davenant's Macbeth dies with these words on his lips, "Farewell vain world, and what's most vain in it Ambition."[9] In Shakespeare's play, Macbeth's final realization is not about ambition, but time. Davenant reduces the play to a sermon on ambition, as it still remains in many productions today.

Davenant's changes provide us with a lens through which we can better understand Shakespeare's plays. In Davenant, vice and virtue, to use the words he gives to Macduff, are separated by character. In Shakespeare, both are contained in all characters. Everyone can be compromised and in *Macbeth* everyone is compromised.

In *Reinventing Shakespeare*, Gary Taylor writes: "Such adaptations increased from a handful in the 1660s to an actual majority of Shakespeare revivals in the 1690s."[10] Davenant's *Macbeth* continued on the stage for nearly a century. Because Davenant's name did not appear on the title page of his adaptation, David Garrick, the preeminent Shakespearean actor of his day, thought the script he was using was Shakespeare's play. One of the true champions of Shakespeare in the eighteenth century, Garrick "restored" the play in 1744. That restoration still cut a large part of *Macbeth*'s already short text, gave the dying Macbeth a new speech, and retained "some of Davenant's scenic and musical elaborations in the witches' scenes."[11] The unedited text of Shakespeare's play with the murder of Macduff's son onstage was not used until 1850.

Lear gets a happy ending

Other Restoration adaptations of Shakespeare's plays held the stage for an even longer period of time and with similar damage. Davenant's "reshaping of *Hamlet* satisfies a neoclassical preference for unambiguous heroes and villains, for moral as well as structural clarity and contrast."[12] Perhaps the most notorious Restoration adaptation is Nahum Tate's version of *Lear*. He removed the Fool and gave Lear and Cordelia a happy ending. This version of *Lear* and the Davenant/Dryden *Tempest* held the stage until William Charles Macready restored Shakespeare's originals in 1838. Macready became a leading advocate for returning to Shakespeare's texts, but old adaptations were still performed. A restored *King Lear* did not reach American stages until the 1870s. Many of Davenant's changes to *Hamlet* survived even longer.

Colley Cibber's version of *Richard III* (1700) became one of the most performed of Shakespeare texts. It narrowed the focus to the title character, cut the characters of Margaret and Clarence, and gave Richard seven additional soliloquies. Remarkably, Cibber presented Richard *in love*, first with Anne and then with Elizabeth. This version held the stage until Henry Irving returned to Shakespeare's text in 1877.[13] It lives on in part in Laurence Olivier's 1955 film version, where Cibber is acknowledged in the screen credits.

Garrick may have "restored" *Macbeth*, but he substantially altered *Romeo and Juliet*. He did not understand that Shakespeare uses Romeo's verbal excesses to characterize him and so edited his language. The most stunning change, however, comes when Romeo, in his first scene, declares his love not for Rosaline, but for Juliet. Garrick explained the reason in his introduction to the published edition in 1750: "When this play was reviv'd two Winters ago it was generally thought, that the sudden Change of Romeo's Love from Rosaline to Juliet was a Blemish in his character."[14] That blemish, of course, is that Shakespeare understands that the affections of a teenage boy can turn suddenly because he is at an age when love and lust blur. You can still see that sanitized moon-eyed lover as late as Franco Zeffirelli's 1968 film.

The emphasis in these adaptations on leading characters was perpetuated by the actors/managers who ran their theatres and played the leads. Shakespeare's plays were expansive in part because he could afford to be expansive. He wrote for a large company of actors. Many productions of the Scottish play flounder because of the lack of a strong ensemble. *Macbeth* needs more than two strong actors: it needs a star company.

What is the legacy of these adaptations? Shakespeare's plays were simplified to studies of their leading characters and their tragic flaws. We still hear these phrases today: Macbeth is ambitious; Hamlet indecisive; *Othello* a warning against jealousy. Minor characters and scenes are cut, eliminating the content of those scenes and their contribution, usually to the public story of the plays. The historical and societal impulses behind the writing of the plays were lost. Davenant's *Macbeth* led to a series of false notions about that play that we can still find in productions today: that the Macbeths are evil, rather than become evil; that the play focuses on ambition, rather than how they descend into evil; and that Macduff is the play's hero, rather than a part of a compromised group of characters that unites under the leadership of Malcolm to remove Macbeth's regime. Davenant's reductions also background two public stories that are still relevant today. One examines the nature of leadership; the other, how uncertainty, fear, and cowardice extend the life of oppressive governments. Such adaptations had a pernicious effect on our perceptions of Shakespeare's plays. The most popular suffered the most because they were the most often adapted and produced. Among them was *Macbeth*.

Notes

1 Andrew Gurr, *The Shakespearean Stage, 1574–1642* (Cambridge, 1980), p. 143. An excellent history of the development of Elizabethan and Jacobean stages and the buildings that housed them.
2 Gary Taylor, *Reinventing Shakespeare* (Weidenfeld & Nicolson, 1989), p. 13. An excellent, comprehensive study of the reinvention of Shakespeare's plays over the centuries.
3 Ibid., p. 45.
4 John Dryden, "Preface to Troilus and Cressida," in *The Essays of Dryden*, ed. W. P. Ker (Oxford Clarendon, 1926), Vol. 1, p. 215 [as cited in Dennis Bartholomeusz, *Macbeth and the Players* (Cambridge, 1969), p. 21, footnote 3].
5 Christopher Spencer, *Davenant's Macbeth from the Yale Manuscript* (Yale, 1961), 3.2.5–6.
6 Ibid., 5.7.123–24.
7 Ibid., 4.4.45–57.
8 Ibid., 1.7.1–6.
9 Ibid., 5.7.83.
10 Taylor, *Reinventing Shakespeare*, p. 20.
11 Ibid., p. 120.
12 Ibid., p. 48.
13 Ibid., pp. 200–1.
14 *Romeo and Juliet*, ed. David Garrick (Cornmarket Press, 1969), p. A3.

Bibliography

Bartholomeusz, Dennis. *Macbeth and the Players*. Cambridge, 1969.
Garrick, David, ed. *Romeo and Juliet*. Cornmarket Press, 1969.
Gurr, Andrew. *The Shakespearean Stage, 1574–1642*. Cambridge, 1980.
Spencer, Christopher. *Davenant's Macbeth from the Yale Manuscript*. Yale, 1961.
Taylor, Gary. *Reinventing Shakespeare*. Weidenfeld & Nicolson, 1989.

13 Crime and punishment

As we return to the private story of the Macbeths, a quick look at the trajectory of their scenes together reveals a pattern to their evolving relationship. They have three scenes before Duncan's murder is discovered. All are duets and in them the Macbeths plan and execute Duncan's murder. In this part of the play, we see them onstage together only in private conversations. Each also has a public scene with the court: Duncan and Macbeth, when he returns from the battlefield; Lady Macbeth and Duncan, when he enters her castle.

After Duncan's murder, the Macbeths are seen together in three large public scenes. The first occurs when the court gathers after Duncan's murder; the two other court scenes are placed before and after Banquo is murdered. In this section of the play, the Macbeths have only two duets, and the second, which follows the banquet in which Banquo's ghost appears, is only one page long. The progression of their eight scenes together suggests a movement away from the focus on their extraordinary intimacy.

Shakespeare shows us that change at the end of the court scene that begins Act Three.

Modern editions rearrange the Folio's irregular lineation in Macbeth's dismissal of the court in various ways. The Bedford / St. Martin's edition rearranges the lines into standard blank verse, which I believe conceals Shakespeare's intention:

> Let every man be master of his time
> Till seven at night. To make society
> The sweeter welcome, we will keep ourself
> Till suppertime alone. While then, God be with you![1]

The Oxford edition I have been quoting makes only one change in the Folio's lineation and adds dashes to isolate a sentence, which I believe reveals Shakespeare's intention:

> Let every man be master of his time
> Till seven at night –

To make society the sweeter welcome,
We will keep ourself till supper-time alone –
While then, God be with you.[2]

Dashes can indicate a change in the person addressed. There is only one person present who needs this explanation [italics added]: "To make society the sweeter welcome, / We will keep ourself till supper-time *alone*." Macbeth is asking his wife to leave. There are two dismissals here, and the second is to her. Macbeth will plan the next round of murders for the first time without her in the scene that follows. The two short lines give him beats to turn his focus to and from her. Shakespeare creates a major turning point in their relationship without giving her the opportunity to question her dismissal in front of the court.

Lady Macbeth acknowledges this when next she greets him in private. She repeats the key word in that dismissal: "How now, my Lord, why do you keep *alone* [italics added]?"[3] She goes on to try to ease his state of mind: "what's done, is done." However, unlike his wife, Macbeth has the ability to anticipate the future and replies, "We have scorched the snake, not killed it."[4] Later in the scene, she asks a direct question: "What's to be done?" He evades answering by reassuring her – and us – of his love for her: "Be innocent of the knowledge, dearest chuck, / Till thou applaud the deed."[5]

Why does Macbeth stop sharing his plans with her? This is a question that I have seldom seen addressed in productions, let alone answered. In Shakespeare, the answer is usually found in what has gone before. It may be in the preceding lines; it can also be in a preceding action. In the chaotic public scene that follows Duncan's murder, Lady Macbeth faints. That faint is most often seen today as a pretense, an attempt to divert those present from Macbeth's disarray. This creates an effective dramatic moment for this strong woman, which makes it a tempting choice. If the faint is real, however, and comes not as a cover for his disarray but from her distress over it, that provides a reason for Macbeth's decision to remove her from his planning. Macbeth will now take the lead in order to protect the woman he loves – his "dearest chuck," who does not anticipate the consequences of their actions – from the knowledge of the necessity for more murders.

Traditions in presenting Lady Macbeth have obscured the full beauty of her conception. Neither her need to invoke spirits to unsex her, nor her admission that she loved the "babe" she would have killed, nor her excuse that she would have killed Duncan herself had he not resembled her father, nor her faint – none of these mitigate her remarkable fierceness and will. They do argue for a more complex character than is usually presented and one that prepares us for her state in the sleepwalking scene. After all, it is she, not he, who goes mad and commits suicide. From her first scene, Shakespeare shows us a series of cracks in her celebrated armor, but traditions in presenting her onstage have blinded us to taking them into account.

The first reason Macbeth stops sharing plans is because of her; the second is because of him. After Macbeth tells her to "be innocent of the knowledge," Lady Macbeth watches her husband deliver a speech that echoes her earlier "Come you spirits" invocation.[6] *His* invocation demonstrates to her and to us just how much he has changed:

> . . . Come, seeling night,
> Scarf up the tender eye of pitiful day,
> And with thy bloody and invisible hand
> Cancel and tear to pieces that great bond
> Which keeps me pale . . .
> – Thou marvell'st at my words; but hold thee still.
> Things bad begun make strong themselves by ill –
> So prithee go with me.[7]

"Thou marvell'st at my words" contains an unwritten stage direction: she is shocked to hear him talk in this fashion. At the end of this and their next scene together, there are two other unwritten stage directions. Lady Macbeth is so stunned by the change in his demeanor that he must beckon her to exit in each scene: "Prithee go with me," at the end of his speech above, and "Come, we'll to sleep."[8] It is Macbeth who now leads the way.

Macbeth has been a good student. He has absorbed his wife's function and he no longer needs her to commit his crimes. In the soliloquy that precedes his scene with Banquo's murderers, Macbeth talks himself into the next round of murders by raising the subject of children, as Lady Macbeth did with him at the end of Act One. When the murderers enter, Macbeth challenges their manhood to bully them into doing his bidding, as his wife did to him earlier.[9] Mary Shelley would approve: the monster no longer needs his creator, or perhaps more accurately, the monster was sleeping. Lady Macbeth, like Queen Mab, is not the creator but the midwife of his dreams.

His last line to her in the entire play is at the end of their short duet following the third act banquet, and it is the play's most chilling: "We are yet but young indeed."[10] Macbeth understands, as she does not, what lies ahead. The Folio uses the word *indeed*, but the eighteenth-century editor Theobald was right in making the pun clearer, and Kenneth Muir follows Theobald in his Arden edition: "We are yet but young in deed."[11]

As with Malcolm and Macduff, the Macbeths are a deadly team: they complement and complete each other. Ironically, in their complicated relationship, Shakespeare gives us his most nearly perfect married couple in their love, understanding, and support for each other. The terrible act of murder, however, separates them and dooms their relationship. Lady Macbeth leaves the play in the sleepwalking scene, as she entered it – alone. That word appears in the Folio's stage direction on her first entrance. It is echoed in the lines cited earlier. She leaves the play alone as well, entirely unaware of the two other people in the room. The series of lines that begin with "What's done, is done," and continues with "What's to be done?" is hauntingly rephrased in her penultimate line in the play: "What's done, cannot be undone."[12]

Anthony Brennan stresses the progressive isolation of the Macbeths which becomes important to understanding the play they dominate. He writes: "Nowhere else does Shakespeare undertake this feat of locking two major characters almost entirely into their *own* personal hells [italics added]."[13] Their isolation from each other is the ultimate punishment they pay for their crimes. They are not seen together in the last two acts of the play.

Equivocation carries a steep price. The deception that it requires has led our murderers into isolation first from their community, and then as described above from each other, and gradually from their own selves: Lady Macbeth's madness and suicide is the ultimate manifestation of the physical and spiritual disembodiment needed to commit murder. Her death leaves Macbeth alone as well, and encourages him to plunge headlong into his. One action leads inexorably to another: these six words are both the essence of drama and of Shakespeare's dramaturgy *and* vision here. And why this tightly constructed play is one of the summits of theatre.

The shock of recognition

I first understood the power of Shakespeare's plays when I saw Peter Brooks's production of *A Midsummer Night's Dream* in 1971.[14] It was the first time I experienced the shock of recognition in the theatre. I faced an uncomfortable truth for a young man who was smitten at the time: when love is not there, there is nothing you can do about it – unless the gods intervene.

Thornton Wilder talks about this kind of recognition in the passage from *3 Plays by Wilder*, part of which I quoted earlier:

> The response we make when we "believe" a work of the imagination is that of saying: "This is the way things are. I have always known it without being fully aware that I knew it. Now in the presence of this play, or novel or poem (or picture or piece of music) I know that I know it." It is

> this form of knowledge which Plato called "recollection." We have all murdered, in thought; and been murdered. We have all seen the ridiculous in estimable persons and in ourselves. We have all known terror as well as enchantment. Imaginative literature has nothing to say to those who do not recognize – who cannot be *reminded* – of such conditions.[15]

So much has been written about the formal elements of Brooks's production. Its stunningly simple white-walled set was an extraordinary choice for a play largely set in the woods and at night; its use of circus elements created the magical realm of the fairies. The dress in *Midsummer* was not modern, but its simplicity helped make the characters immediately recognizable. By doing this, Brook blew away the literal trappings that too often obscure *Midsummer*. As a result, he was able to filter the play through a third time period that we must always observe. The period in which we live is always the lens through which we view Shakespeare's plays. By stripping away clichés, Brook revealed the human dramas in the play: the sense of betrayal behind Oberon and Titania's confrontations, the pain of the mismatched lovers, Bottom's loneliness. He understood that Shakespeare does not judge his characters and so Brook respected their pain, even as we laughed at their situations. Brook gave us, for example, a Helena who was alas too tall, too smart, and too shy to be desirable to many young men of her world – or ours. Before speaking her first lines, the actress who played her, Frances de la Tour, entered the stage with bounding energy, but withdrew immediately into herself when she saw others in the room. That one image conveyed with clarity and complexity both her vitality and the reality that it had already been thwarted.

Shakespeare draws on the deeper potentialities of theatre. Wilder writes on this subject in the essay I quoted above: "I began to feel that the [contemporary] theatre was not only inadequate, it was evasive; it did not wish to draw on its deeper potentialities. I found the word for it: it aimed to be *soothing*. The tragic had no heat; the comic had no bite; the social criticism failed to indict us with responsibility."[16]

Brook gave me something that too often is missing in productions of Shakespeare's comedies – recognition of the human drama underneath. In doing so, Brook held up a mirror in which I was able to recognize myself. Shakespeare's great gift is that he allows us to see ourselves in others by finding the universal in the particular.

Uncomfortable truths

If you want to truly understand Shakespeare's plays, you must rise to his level of sophistication about people, including the paradoxes in their character. In Act Five, Shakespeare gives Macbeth a soliloquy that pulls us back into seeing the play from his perspective. It is a human reaction to his wife's death, and it reminds us of Macbeth's lingering humanity and exposes the nihilism to which this magnificent mind has sunk:

> She should have died hereafter;
> There would have been a time for such a word –
> Tomorrow, and tomorrow, and tomorrow,
> Creeps in this petty pace from day to day,
> To the last syllable of recorded time;
> And all our yesterdays have lighted fools
> The way to dusty death. Out, out, brief candle,
> Life's but a walking shadow, a poor player
> That struts and frets his hour upon the stage,
> And then is heard no more. It is a tale
> Told by an idiot, full of sound and fury
> Signifying nothing.[17]

Who is the idiot? The logic of the play seems to point to Macbeth, and to all of us who believe we can control the future and discover too late that we can only control the choices we make. But even generous choices in this play have unintended consequences. Macbeth tries to protect his wife and that leads to their isolation from each other and eventually to her death. Understood in this context, Macbeth's soliloquy is an angry outcry against the universe and the idiot is God. Does "Tomorrow, and tomorrow, and tomorrow" lead to enlightenment or to cynicism? For Macbeth, perhaps enlightenment is cynicism. That is the paradox to which Shakespeare leads Macbeth at the end of his play. As Jan Kott suggests, "All he has left is contempt. . . . All he can do is to drag with him into nothingness as many living beings as possible."[18]

As for us, Shakespeare lets you decide. Art exists in the *interaction* between the work of art and the viewer/listener/reader. Each member of the audience quite naturally brings his or her life and times to what they see onstage. Shakespeare's remarkable dramaturgy poses questions and allows us to personalize our experience of the wide canvass of his plays through the issues that are the most powerful for each of us. That is his deep understanding of the nature of theatre and where the power of his dramaturgy ultimately lies. This gives his plays the elasticity to embrace a wide audience over many centuries. That embrace, however, is fatal: it allows Shakespeare to draw us into his plays and then take us on a journey that implicates us with the shock of recognition. In *Midsummer*, that skill consoles us: that is why it is a comedy. In *Macbeth*, that skill indicts us.

This can only happen if, as Wilder points out, we are willing to recognize ourselves in others. That is the ultimate act of recognition that we must bring to the table. In *Macbeth*, Shakespeare asks us to embrace the *struggles* of his leading characters, even when we would rather keep a comfortable distance from them. The process of mounting or viewing Shakespeare's plays is a journey of both discovery and self-discovery. To paraphrase the great art critic Robert Hughes on Goya: "To meet Shakespeare is still to meet ourselves."[19] I would add this: to meet ourselves is to meet Shakespeare. If you truly want to understand Shakespeare's plays, you must look in a mirror as well as in his "Book." Addressing the third time period means confronting the Porter's question, "What are you?"

Notes

1 *Macbeth*, ed. William C. Carroll (Bedford/St. Martin's, 1999), 3.1.42–45. Note that there is an extra foot in the last line.
2 *Macbeth*, ed. Nicholas Brooke (Oxford World Classics, 2014), 3.1.40–44.
3 Ibid., 3.2.9.
4 Ibid., 3.2.13–14.
5 Ibid., 3.2.47–48.
6 Ibid.,1.5.39–53.
7 Ibid., 3.2.49–59.
8 Ibid., 3.4.143.
9 Ibid., 1.7.47–51.
10 Ibid., 3.4.145.
11 *Macbeth*, ed. Kenneth Muir, Arden Second Series (Methuen, 1951), 3.4.145.
12 *Macbeth*, ed. Nicholas Brooke, 3.2.13 and 47, and 5.1.65.
13 Anthony Brennan, *Shakespeare's Dramatic Structures* (Routledge, 1986), p. 121.
14 The American tour on Broadway of the Royal Shakespeare Company's celebrated production.
15 Thornton Wilder, "Introduction," in *Three Plays* (Harper Perennial Modern Classics, 2006), pp. XXV–XXVI.
16 Ibid., p. XXVI.
17 *Macbeth*, ed. Nicholas Brooke, 5.5.17–28.
18 Jan Kott, *Shakespeare Our Contemporary* (Norton, 1974), p. 97.
19 From the end of Robert Hughes' 1999 televised program, *Goya*: *Crazy Like a Genius*: "To meet Goya is still to meet ourselves." BBC, 1999.

Bibliography

Shakespeare editions cited

Macbeth. Ed. Kenneth Muir, Arden Second Edition. Methuen, 1951.
Macbeth. Ed. Nicholas Brooke. Oxford World Classics, 1994.
Macbeth. Ed. William C. Carroll. Bedford/St. Martin's, 1999.
The Norton Facsimile: *The First Folio of Shakespeare*. Ed. Charlton Hinman. Norton, 1968.

Other sources

Brennan, Anthony. *Shakespeare's Dramatic Structures*. Routledge, 1986.
Hughes, Robert. *Goya*: *Crazy Like a Genius*. BBC, 1999.
Kott, Jan. *Shakespeare Our Contemporary*. Norton, 1964.
Wilder, Thornton. *Three Plays*. Harper Perennial Modern Classics, 2006.

Coda

Does Shakespeare need a facelift?

My favorite audience for *Romeo and Juliet* at Stratford Canada in 2008 was a group of high school students who sat through a performance that was three hours and fifteen minutes long, and who cheered at the end. Later that year, when they were planning a school production of *A Midsummer Night's Dream*, they asked their teacher if they could perform that play in contemporary language as we did in *Romeo and Juliet*. The language in our production, however, was largely unchanged and uncut. We even included the musicians' scene.

I think of this as I read an article in a 2015 *Wall Street Journal* about the Oregon Shakespeare Festival's project of "translating" Shakespeare plays for modern audiences and James Shapiro's impassioned Op-Ed page response to that idea in the *New York Times*.[1] I have friends among the translators and no wish to criticize such serious theatre artists on work that I have not seen or had the opportunity to read. As of the writing of this book, that work has not yet been produced.[2] The project, however, is part of a long history of changing Shakespeare's texts, and I would like to frame some of the challenges those translators face in that context, in order to express some final thoughts on the nature of Shakespeare's dramaturgy.

Shakespeare's words were changed as early as the printing of the First Folio. When the compositors who set the type had difficulty reading the handwritten manuscripts, they chose words that made sense to them, if not always to us today. Perhaps the most notorious example comes from the compositor dubbed the Apprentice because his choices often were obviously questionable. The phrase that in *Hamlet* Q2 appears as "O treble woe" was printed as "Oh terrible woer" in the Folio passage the Apprentice set.[3] Fortunately, other compositors usually made better substitutions. Unfortunately, that made their substitutions more difficult to detect. I find these Folio changes instructive because they demonstrate that it is easy to spot the questionable choice. Four hundred years later, it is much more difficult to identify the seemingly reasonable substitutions that may change the meaning of a passage or even an entire play.

The Folio substitutions were unwitting mistakes, but the many changes that subsequent editors and adaptors made were deliberate, often to address the aesthetics of their times. In his 1725 edition, the poet Alexander Pope began the task of collating folio and quarto texts. Some of the latter were just being rediscovered. Unfortunately, Pope "freely reworked any material he didn't like [and] discarded passages he thought unworthy. . . . Where, for instance, Shakespeare wrote about taking arms against a sea of troubles, he changed *sea* to *siege* to avoid a mixed metaphor."[4] Pope changed a word to conform to the taste of his times, but in doing so altered the idea in Shakespeare's phrase.

What follows is a hypothetical example of word substitutions that would have more serious consequences, and in ways that may not be readily apparent. These are the opening lines of Macbeth's soliloquy in 1.7:

> . . . if th'assassination
> Could trammel up the consequence and catch
> With his [Duncan's] surcease, success, that but this blow
> Might be the be-all and the end-all . . .
> We'd jump the life to come. But in these cases
> We still have judgment here, that we but teach
> Bloody instructions, which being taught, return
> To plague th'inventor . . .[5]

Surcease means "the *act* of bringing . . . to an end."[6] It is used in legal proceedings and leads us to the key word "judgment" later in the passage. Macbeth is referring to Duncan's murder, but he does not use that word. In this soliloquy and the dialogue that follows, Macbeth uses "murderer" once to argue *against* his committing that act, but he avoids saying the word *murder* six times. He begins with the most charged word, *assassination*, but continues with terms that are progressively more neutral: *surcease* and *blow*, as quoted above, and later in the soliloquy and the lines that follow, *deed*, *taking-off*, and *business*. Macbeth is still vacillating about the decision to murder Duncan and his choice of words tells us that. When Macbeth finally stops hesitating, he will say murder in an unqualified manner for the first time in the dagger speech,[7] and then proceed with it. His reluctance to do so earlier suggests that he is not yet the "butcher" that he is called by Malcolm at the end of the play[8] – and which many productions make him out to be from the beginning. To change *surcease* or the other words cited above to *murder* would change who Macbeth is at this point and Shakespeare's play itself. Words matter in Shakespeare.

As discussed in Chapter 12, wholesale adaptations of Shakespeare's texts for performance began during the Restoration period and contained even more substantial changes. We rarely produce these adaptations today because their limitations are evident and serious. Unfortunately, these adaptations changed our perception of Shakespeare's plays in ways that are sometimes difficult to refute today because of our reverence for the false performance traditions they engendered.

In addition to these concerns, the more experience I have with changing the texts of Shakespeare's plays, the more I understand how dangerous it is to alter poetry. This is an aspect of Shakespeare's writing that is difficult for us to appreciate fully today at a time when poetry sadly has receded in popular discourse and we have less understanding of its full dimensions. In a chapter from *The Well Wrought Urn* entitled "The Heresy of Paraphrase," Cleanth Brooks uses *Macbeth* as one of the ten works (and the only play) to make observations about poetry, two of which are particularly relevant to Shakespeare. The first is applicable to the ambiguity and paradox that are characteristic of Shakespeare's plays:

> Where is the dictionary which contains the terms of a poem? It is a truism that the poet is continually forced to remake language. As [T. S.] Eliot has put it, his task is to "dislocate language into meaning" . . . the word, as the poet uses it, has to be conceived of, not as a discrete particle of meaning, but as a potential of meaning, a nexus or cluster of meanings.[9]

Brooks also makes a second point that is essential to understanding Shakespeare's dramaturgy. Brooks sees poetry as kin to a play in that both are dynamic, "an *experience* rather than any mere statement about experience [italics added]."[10] An experience moves us beyond the reductive and static realm of statement into the interactive and progressive complexity that is the realm of art.

I have never worked on a production of a Shakespeare play where we have not changed some words in the expectation of making the thoughts clearer, and this can open up a scene, as the Porter demonstrates. I have also seen how an actor can illuminate obscure words and guide the audience through difficult passages *if* that actor understands the meanings of those words. I believe the real problem we face when we work on Shakespeare's plays is a lack of time, both in preparation and rehearsals. Those students I cited at the beginning of this section thought we had updated the language of *Romeo and Juliet* because we were fortunate enough at Stratford to have the time to investigate the meanings of Shakespeare's words and to discover why each scene was there.

Unfortunately, time usually requires money that, too often, is not there. The lack of resources defeats many productions of plays that bear

Shakespeare's name. Because we had the time at Stratford, we were able to communicate the simple and often hard beauty of Shakespeare's plays. I use that word as John Keats used it in another poem that Brooks examines in his book. That poem ends with these words: " 'Beauty is truth, truth beauty,' – that is all / Ye know on earth, and all ye need to know."[11]

What is truth in Shakespeare? In his Foreword to this book, McAnuff writes these words: Shakespeare "managed to create a matrix of points of view without seeming to judge the individuals that he was portraying . . . a theatrical blueprint for life itself." That is the hard beauty of his plays, and it is the relentless and ineluctable tomorrow Shakespeare so powerfully illustrates in Macbeth which will tell us if the Oregon project brings us closer to realizing that.

Notes

1 John H. McWhorter, "A Facelift for Shakespeare," *Wall Street Journal*, September 25, 2015; James Shapiro, "Shakespeare in Modern English?" *New York Times*, October 7, 2015.
2 Shapiro had access to the first Oregon translation, *Timon of Athens*.
3 The Norton Facsimile: *The First Folio of Shakespeare*, ed. Charlton Hinman (Norton, 1968), p. XIX.
4 Bill Bryson, *Shakespeare: The World as Stage* (Atlas Books, 2007), p. 173.
5 *Macbeth*, ed. Nicholas Brooke (Oxford World Classics, 2014), 1.7.2–12.
6 *Oxford English Dictionary* (Oxford University Press, 1971), surcease: sb. 1 and 3.
7 Macbeth uses the word *murder* in a qualified way earlier at 1.3.39, where he calls his *thought* of murder "but fantastical." He finally says *murder* at 2.1.52.
8 *Macbeth*, ed. Nicholas Brooke (Oxford World Classics, 2014), 5.7.99.
9 Cleanth Brooks, "The Naked Babe and the Cloak of Manliness," in *The Well Wrought Urn* (Harcourt Brace, 1947), p. 210.
10 Ibid., p. 213.
11 John Keats, "Ode to a Grecian Urn," in *The Poems of John Keats*, ed. Jack Stillinger (Harvard University, 1978), p. 373.

Bibliography

Shakespeare editions cited

Macbeth. Ed. Nicholas Brooke. Oxford World Classics, 1994.
The Norton Facsimile: *The First Folio of Shakespeare*. Ed. Charlton Hinman. Norton, 1968.

Other sources

Brooks, Cleanth. *The Well Wrought Urn*. Harcourt Brace, 1947.
Bryson, Bill. *Shakespeare: The World as Stage*. Atlas Books, 2007.

Keats, John. *The Poems of John Keats*, Ed. Jack Stillinger. Harvard University Press, 1978.

McWhorter, John H. "A Facelift for Shakespeare." *Wall Street Journal*, September 25, 2015.

Oxford English Dictionary. Oxford University Press, 1971.

Shapiro, James. "Shakespeare in Modern English?" *New York Times*, October 7, 2015.

Index

For Product Safety Concerns and Information please contact our EU representative GPSR@taylorandfrancis.com Taylor & Francis Verlag GmbH, Kaufingerstraße 24, 80331 München, Germany

Printed and bound by CPI Group (UK) Ltd, Croydon, CR0 4YY
11/04/2025
01844008-0008